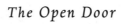

The Open Door

Other books by Frederica Mathewes-Green

Real Choices: Listening to Women,
Looking for Alternatives to Abortion

Facing East: A Pilgrim's Journey into the
Mysteries of Orthodoxy

At the Corner of East and Now:
A Modern Life in Ancient Christian Orthodoxy

Gender: Men, Women, Sex, Feminism

The companion to this volume is

The Illumined Heart:
The Ancient Christian Path of
Transformation

The Open Door

Entering the Sanctuary of Icons and Prayer

FREDERICA
MATHEWES-GREEN

PARACLETE PRESS
Brewster, Massachusetts

With grateful appreciation to St. Isaac of Syria Skete of Boscobel,
Wisconsin, for providing the images in this book

St. Isaac of Syria Skete
25266 Pilgrim's Way, Boscobel, Wisconsin 53805
Ph 800-81-ICONS   www.skete.com

Scripture quotations are taken from the Revised Standard
Version of the Bible, copyright 1946, 1952, 1971 by the
Division of Christian Education of the National Council of the
Churches of Christ in the USA. Used by permission.

Published in association with the literary agency of
Alive Communications, Inc., 7680 Goddard Street, Suite 200,
Colorado Springs, Colorado 80920.

Library of Congress Cataloging-in-Publication Data

Mathewes-Green, Frederica.
    The open door: entering the sanctuary of icons and prayer /
Frederica Mathewes-Green.
      p. cm.   (Paraclete pocket faith series)
Includes bibliographical references.
      ISBN 1-55725-341-2 (hardcover)
      1. Icons—Cult—Meditations. 2. Orthodox Eastern
Church—Prayer-books and devotions—English.
I. Title. II. Series.
      BX378.5.M38 2003
      246'.53—dc21   2003011538
              10 9 8 7 6 5 4 3 2 1

© 2003 by Frederica Mathewes-Green

ISBN 1-55725-341-2

PUBLISHED BY PARACLETE PRESS
Brewster, Massachusetts
www.paracletepress.com

Printed in the United States of America.

To David Benjamin, Hannah, Isaac, Adam,
and all the grandbabies still to come.

CONTENTS

ILLUSTRATIONS

PART 1

The Iconostasis

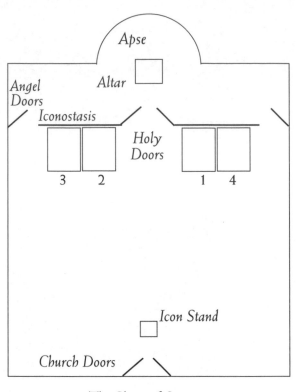

1 The Christ of Sinai
2 The Virgin of Vladimir
3 The Resurrection
4 John the Baptist

PLAN OF THE CHURCH

CHAPTER ONE

The Christ of Sinai

Unless you're a member of an Orthodox church, you probably haven't encountered icons in their natural setting. You may have seen them in magazines or museums and wondered at their mysterious and somewhat forbidding quality.

When I became an Orthodox Christian, icons were one of the hardest things for me to get used to. They didn't seem very friendly. They didn't even seem like good art. Gradually, though, I learned that icons are not intended to be art-book pictures. They're companions in prayer, both public worship and private devotion. I hope in this book to help you encounter icons in that larger context and understand what role they play.

We'll do this by visiting an imaginary church at various times during the year, meeting the icons "at work" there, and getting to know them better. In some churches the interior will be nearly covered with icons,

3

and the sight can be visually overwhelming. We'll try to simplify things by turning our attention to two different areas of the church. In Part I of the book we'll be looking at the icons on the iconostasis, a wooden screen that stands before the altar area. The color panels at the center of the book represent the four major icons on the iconostasis. We'll examine these icons, and address the larger questions about icons and their place in the life of faith, in Part I of this book.

In Part II we'll turn to the black-and-white icons in the book's center. These will serve to represent the icons placed on a small stand just inside the church door, which are changed to correspond with the feasts of the Church year.

A book this small cannot, of course, be a comprehensive guide to icons, but I trust it will be a useful introduction. Through it I hope you will begin to know icons and discover ways that they can be a part of your own life of prayer. When you visit other churches or meet icons in other contexts, you will be able to recognize them as new friends.

Come in. I want you to see these icons.

We've come into this church around noon on Sunday. The service has recently ended, and the once-feathery wisps of incense are settling into a diffuse pale-gray cloud. It smells like smoke and roses. A few bulletins and worship books are scattered about, and a child's white cardigan lies forgotten under a chair. The church is empty; the congregation has gone downstairs to coffee hour, and we can faintly hear the hubbub of their voices. Up here, though, it's quiet.

Walk up to the center of the church with me and look around. There's a lot to take in. The church looks surprisingly complicated inside, compared to how it looked when we were coming up the sidewalk. From the outside it looked like a simple cube. But in here much of the walls and even ceiling have been covered with paintings of people and scenes from the Bible and Church history. It's initially bewildering to the eye, with so many stories and scenes going on at once.

But if you imagine the room painted solid white you can see that it's still a cube, with a

5

single large dome centered overhead. If you look toward the back wall, behind the altar, you'll see that it is topped with a half-dome, what architects call an *apse*. This altar area is separated from the main body of the church by a wooden screen, the *iconostasis*. And that's it, actually. There aren't even pews, only a few short rows of chairs against the walls. During worship, most of the congregation stands clustered on the oriental rugs in the center. (A floor plan of our imaginary church appears on page 2).

Unlike the familiar kind of pointy church that sends a steeple soaring toward the heavens, this dome covers worshipers as with a bowl. It conveys a feeling of God joining us in the Incarnation and rounding us into one Body.

When the congregation first moved into this building the walls were bare white, and the congregation has been saving up to add made-to-order icons a few at a time, as they can afford to have them painted. Some of the prime spots in the church don't yet have hand-painted icons. In those places the congregation is using reproductions of classic icons that have been laminated onto wooden panels. All the icons we will be looking at in this book fall into that category of historic reproduction.[1]

Let's look at the iconostasis, that wooden screen before the altar. The Greek word means "icon-stand." On it is set a series of large, almost life-size icons. Fold out the color panel and you'll see two icons on each side. On the iconostasis these four icons are side-by-side in this order. In the middle, between the Virgin Mary and Christ, there is an elaborate double door that opens to the altar, called the *Holy Doors*. The key on page 2 will help you visualize the arrangement.

On these doors there is an icon of the Angel Gabriel announcing the birth of the Christ Child to the Virgin Mary. Beyond these doors is the altar, and behind the altar, on the back wall of the church, is the apse we noticed earlier. The apse is filled with a very large icon of the Virgin Mary standing with her hands raised in prayer. On her torso

[1] I am grateful to St. Isaac of Syria Skete of Boscobel, Wisconsin, www.skete.com, for supplying these images.

there is a starry disk, and in it we see the Christ Child blessing us.

To the right of those double doors on the iconostasis is the imposing icon of Christ we see reproduced on the back of the color panel. He is holding a jeweled book in one hand and blessing us with the other. His face, and particularly his eyes, are powerfully attractive, compelling, yet also somehow disturbing. They make us feel confused or self-conscious, as if they are asking a question we don't understand.

To the left of the double doors (on the front of the color panel), we recognize the Virgin Mary, who is embracing the Christ Child. She traditionally holds this place on an iconostasis, to Christ's right, recalling the Scripture, "at your right hand stands the queen" (Ps. 45:9). In front of each of these icons is a brass stand holding clusters of beeswax candles, which are now more than half-melted and running with honey-scented streaks. The candles cast flickering light on the figures. These images of Christ and the Virgin are two of the best-known and most beloved icons in the world. We'll be looking at them in this chapter and the next, and learning more of the "what" and "why" of icons.

In the third chapter we will turn to the icon to the left of the Virgin, which shows Christ pulling an old man out of a tomb, while other figures stand behind him in a rocky landscape. The old man is our fore-father Adam, and this icon represents the events of Holy Saturday, when Christ went into the realm of Death and set the captives free. This spot on an iconostasis is usually reserved for the saint or feast for whom a church is named, so now we know that this church is called Holy Resurrection.

On the far right side of the iconostasis (on the back of the colored panel) we see a man looking toward Christ and lifting his hands in imploring prayer. We could guess from his disheveled appearance that this is St. John the Baptist, even if we didn't know that this is his usual spot on an iconostasis. We'll get to know him further in the fourth chapter.

If you turn around, you'll see something going on everywhere you look. There are

9

brass candlestands, hanging oil lamps, and a box of sand forested with leaning candle nubs. Toward the front there is a bulky wooden bookstand for the chanters; in the back there are a dozen music stands for the choir. Near the iconostasis there is a large baptismal font shaped like a silver chalice. On the far edges of the iconostasis, beyond the Resurrection and St. John, angels stand guard on doors leading back to the altar. If we look up at the ceiling we're startled to see Christ gazing directly down on us from the dome centered over the nave. Though the congregation has gone downstairs, the church retains a hum of bustling energy. Something vigorous has been going on here, and the high smoky room still reverberates.

The impact of so much iconography can be overwhelming, an effect compounded by the fact that icons don't seem very inviting. Their unsmiling sobriety throws us off initially, and we aren't sure how to relate to them. Let's begin by taking a closer look at the most demanding one, the icon of Christ. This is not the original, of course, but a large reproduction that this congregation has chosen for this spot on their iconostasis, which always holds an icon of Christ. This is an excellent one to study if we're trying to figure out what icons are all about in the first place.

As you compare it with the other three main ones on the iconostasis you'll notice that it differs from them in several ways. It is more realistic, less stylized, for one thing. The icon's background is not gold, but shows a blue sky and a bit of curving architecture. Christ's face is also more natural-looking, more like a portrait. If you have seen Egyptian or Roman paintings from the first centuries A.D.—the ones on mummy cases in museums, for example—you will notice that this icon resembles them in the expressiveness of the wide eyes and the subtle skin tones.

This is the oldest of our four main icons, and in fact is one of the oldest surviving examples of Christian art. It was painted in the middle of the sixth century, and the fineness of the execution suggests that it was produced in the imperial capital of Constantinople. Yet from the time of its execution it has resided far from that busy city, preserved in a distant monastery in the red granite mountains of the Sinai. This isolation is the main reason it survived.

The southern Sinai is a forbidding place. Yet from earliest times Christians have gone there to live dedicated lives of prayer, near the site of the Burning Bush and the mount where Moses received the Law. When Egeria, a Christian woman from Spain, made a pilgrimage through the Holy Land in the fourth century, the Sinai had already been established as a place of prayer. She wrote of her travels: "There were many cells of holy men there, and a church in the place where the [Burning] Bush is."

But the rocky passes were better fit for nomads, and Bedouin tribes regularly attacked the monks. In the sixth century the monks on Mt. Sinai petitioned the Emperor Justinian to build a walled monastery for their protection. Around the year 550 the walls rose forty feet high, and they still stand today. The monastery within them, now named for St. Catherine of Alexandria, has been in continuous operation ever since.

This icon of Christ probably was sent as a gift to the monks when the monastery was first completed. It is of a type called *Pantocrator*, which means "Ruler of All." While many icons show Christ at various points in his earthly life, a Pantocrator icon is timeless, revealing Him as the eternal judge. It is usually a bust-length image, though sometimes He is shown sitting on a throne. His right hand is raised in blessing, and in His left hand is a massive book. Orthodox Christians would recognize this as a Gospel book, the elaborately-bound volume containing only the four Gospels, which is kept on the altar and read aloud by clergy during services. (The Epistles are kept separately in a smaller, plainer book, and their reading is accompanied by less ceremony.) In some Pantocrator icons, as here, the Gospel book is closed; in some it is shown open and inscribed with a text from the Gospels, often the "I am the way" passage (John 14:6), or "Come to Me" (Matt. 11:28).

Most ancient icons are executed in a paint made with egg yolks, called egg tempera. This one, however, uses an older technique called wax encaustic, melted wax mixed with powdered pigments. For long centuries of prayer in that Sinai monastery the smoke of incense and candles darkened it, and this icon was repeatedly overpainted to restore the image, a fate that befalls many icons. Only in 1962 were these layers removed and the original revealed once more.

I find it hard to keep talking in the presence of this icon; it communicates something so profoundly beautiful—tranquil, filled with tender life—that it seems all the earth should keep silence. That's quite a change for me, because for a long time I didn't like icons at all. They didn't appeal to me; they didn't even make sense. When other people talked about how beautiful and moving icons were, I'd arrange my features into a thoughtful, serious expression, but inside I'd be thinking, "I have no idea what they're talking about."

Icons seemed to me the opposite of appealing. The art looked like bad art, with clumsy perspective and unrealistic faces. Worst of all, icons didn't convey emotion. Everyone looked so stiff and unfriendly.

14

When it came to religious art, I much preferred to stroll the halls of the National Gallery of Art and view color-saturated canvases from the Renaissance, full of plump babies and yearning eyes cast upwards. Art that showed people who looked like real people, portrayed in ways that tugged the heartstrings.

That is decidedly what icons do not do. If you're like I was, it takes a while for this icon of Christ to "speak" to you. When it does, it communicates something subtle, very different from the clear, dramatic message you get from a Renaissance canvas.

Look at the icon of Christ again. You may find his gaze unsettling, as if He is looking back at you, or even through you. My husband, a pastor, once received a phone call from a retired humanities professor. The caller said that he was a lifelong atheist and humanist who was mostly ignorant of religion. But then someone had given him a copy of this icon. "When I look at it, I have the sensation that He's looking into my soul," he said. "Before this, I didn't even think there was such a thing as a soul."

The Christ of Sinai has that penetrating effect. We can understand some of the ways this is achieved artistically, but like pulling the petals off a flower, analyzing details won't fully explain the whole.

One way the iconographer has achieved this intense effect is that the perspective is intentionally distorted. Look at the Gospel book; it towers upward, as if we're standing on the street looking up the corner of a sky-scraper. But if you look at the figure of Christ, it's as if we are facing Him squarely, with our head coming up to His chest. What's more, the whole image of Christ gets subtly *wider* as it goes back into the picture. Why is that?

You'll remember from elementary school art lessons that "perspective" means that when you look at a picture of railroad tracks, far in the distance the tracks converge. The place where everything collapses into a tiny spot is called the "vanishing point." That's the rule in most Western painting. A canvas shows a scene as if you're looking into the box of a theater stage, with everything getting smaller as it goes back. That kind of perspective invites you into the frame of the picture, as if you're entering a room and joining the characters there.

With many icons, however, perspective is reversed. Christ's ears and hair are wider than His face. His shoulders seem to go on forever. Things are getting *larger* as they go back, and smaller as they come toward you. This means that the convergence point is *in front of* the picture, right about where you're standing. You're the "vanishing point." From the perspective of heaven we are so small, and if God did not sustain us we would vanish. No wonder you feel like you're standing on the bull's-eye.

Sometimes several different approaches to perspective might be used in the same icon, as here with the differing angles on the Gospel book and Christ. This gives the viewer a general sensation of being off-balance, outside familiar territory. The Cubists used a similar technique to achieve their everything-at-once effect.

Christ's halo also contributes to the sense of things getting larger. The halo was a new development in art, invented by iconographers. We now think of it as a painter's "poetic license," placing a flat golden disk behind a figure's head to indicate special honor. The original intention, however, was to convey a sphere of light encompassing the person's entire head, or in some cases entire body, like the glow around a candle flame in a dark room. The faint red lines on the halo in the Christ of Sinai give it a slight curve, as if it were cup of gold.

Throughout Scripture and Christian history there is a consistent message that God is Light, and those who belong to Him are said to be illumined by His presence. From the earliest centuries Baptism was referred to as "Illumination." The Gospels tell us that when Christ was transfigured on Mt. Tabor His disciples saw Him glow with a light beyond earthly origin. Similar stories are told of many saints—and not only those in the distant past, by the way. This visible glow of the *Uncreated Light*, as the Church Fathers called it, is what a halo intends to represent.

The use of the halo and mixed perspective both make this icon imposing, but the iconographer has done something else here.

Use a piece of paper or index card to cover first one half of the face and then the other. A dramatic difference appears. Let's examine first the right side of the face, then the left.

The face on the right is looking at you in a way you'd rather not have someone look at you. The gaze is more penetrating than is comfortable. It's a little too knowledgeable. However, we soon realize that the expression is not harsh or rejecting. The expression is lively, as if it is in motion. There is even a bit of humor in it, a lift at the corner of the mouth and cheekbone. He might be saying, "Oh, I've got your number." It is a challenging yet friendly expression, and somehow energetic and purposeful. This might be the expression of a surgeon who knows that his efforts are going to be successful, and is now confident that complete healing will be achieved.

Now cover the right side of the face and look at the left. What tranquility is here! The brow is eloquent as the bow of a violin, subtly lifted in tender compassion. This is a listening eye, patient, waiting to receive all we could pour out of our confused and aching hearts.

19

The shadows have fled away, and the face is full of soft light. You could rest a long time here.

When you look at the whole icon again, you understand better why it is unsettling. The iconographer has sought to express a complex truth here, two concepts that are simultaneous but which we, in our limited way, must go over and over in sequence. The truth is that we need both sides of Christ. We need His challenging "surgical" aspect to reveal our sins and bring them to the surface, so that we can wrestle with and overcome them. This is especially true of the sins we dismiss as insignificant and fail to take seriously, like pride, envy, and self-righteousness.

"I know my transgressions, and my sin is ever before me" the repentant King David said (Ps. 51). In all honesty, we may not be able to say that yet; we may not know what murky motivations and fears circulate in our depths. But as we look at this right side of the icon we know that He sees everything. Until we acknowledge and reject our sins, they will go on poisoning us and poisoning our relationships with others. We pray to be given real repentance, so that we can gain the clear-eyed vision of ourselves that Christ already has. He knows us from the deepest inside out, and as we stand on this side of the icon we welcome His searching gaze.

Not that this process of revelation and cleansing is comfortable. It's scary to be known so thoroughly, but it's also a relief. We have never experienced anyone who knows us this well, and yet He loves us completely. As we look at this icon we see how ancient His love is. He was loving us before we ever turned to look into these eyes. He has been loving us a long time, from a Cross two thousand years before we were born. We don't have to improve, or cover up our faults, to earn this love. It has been surrounding us all our lives, waiting for us to receive it. Perhaps that is the meaning of the faint smile. He loves us too much to let us remain as we are, confused and mired in sin, hurting others and ourselves. He will heal us, and His healing is sure.

Our response to such complete and unexpected love feels like surrender—nearly like collapse, after a lifetime of trying to be good enough, clever enough, handsome enough. After such fruitless and exhausting efforts we come to stillness, like the stillness after sobbing for a long time. And now we see the other side of His face in this icon, the quiet side, the listening side. There is great patience here. That's a good thing, since it may take a very long time, a lifetime, to heal all that needs to heal. He is waiting; He is not in any hurry. He will be right here, even when you forget Him and get tangled in your life again, and have to turn around and come back to Him—not once, but over and over again.

I don't know of another icon that is as complex and searching as the Christ of Sinai. It is a universal favorite, and Orthodox Christians keep copies on their desks, at their bedsides, and on the dashboard of their cars. As we stand here in this church we see it on an iconostasis, where worshipers stand during every service and look toward, then away from, those searching eyes. When a person comes to confession, he or she and the priest will stand side-by-side facing this icon. The person will then speak out everything he needs to say, cleansing his soul in the presence of Christ. The priest is there as a witness, and doesn't deliver absolution so much as recognize it, reminding the person that Christ has forgiven him.

Perhaps you see why I say that this is a different kind of message than you receive from a Renaissance painting. People who get acclimated to icons begin to see classic Western religious paintings as accomplished and beautiful, but noisy. In their busy drama those paintings remain earthbound, superficial. Not that the content of such art is superficial; it may provoke deep thoughts or strong empathy. Yet, in a way that's hard to define, icons touch a completely different interior level, something below the hectic arena of thought and emotion. Deeper down there is a place where we first confront life, before we decide what we think or feel about it. That is the intimate place where icons speak. They are companions in prayer and won't make sense outside the context of a surrendered and seeking life. Icons have their fullest impact on those who are saturated in prayer and Scripture, and who participate in the full life of the Church, with all her mysteries, hymns, and worship.

Look at Him again, and let Him look at you. Take your time. You may have things you want to say, and then you might run out of things to say and need just to be silent before Him. This is a quiet, but very deep, icon.

From Psalm 139

O LORD, You have searched me and known me!
You know when I sit down and when I rise up;
You discern my thoughts from afar.
You search out my path and my lying down,
and are acquainted with all my ways.
Even before a word is on my tongue
O LORD, You know it altogether.
You beset me behind and before,
and lay Your hand upon me.
Such knowledge is too wonderful for me;
it is high, and I cannot attain it.

Whither shall I go from Your Spirit?
Or whither shall I flee from Your presence?

If I ascend to heaven, You are there.
If I make my bed in Sheol, You are there.
If I take the wings of the morning
and dwell in the uttermost parts of the sea,
even there Your hand shall lead me,
and Your right hand shall hold me.
If I say, "Let only darkness cover me,
and let the light about me be night,"
even the darkness is not dark to You,
the night is bright as day;
for darkness is as light with You.

For You formed my inward parts,
You knit me together in my mother's womb.
I praise You, for You are fearful and wonderful.
Wonderful are Your works!
You know me right well;
my frame was not hidden from You
when I was being made in secret,
intricately wrought in the depths of the earth.
Your eyes beheld my unformed substance;
in Your book were written, every one of them,
the days that were formed for me,
when as yet there was none of them.

How precious to me are Your thoughts,
  O God!
How vast is the sum of them!
If I would count them,
they are more than the sand.
When I awake, I am still with You.

Search me, O God, and know my heart!
Try me, and know my thoughts!
See if there be any wicked way in me,
and lead me in the way everlasting!

CHAPTER TWO

The Virgin of Vladimir

We've come back to the church on a weeknight in early August. It's hot outside, the jumbled tail end of rush hour, and the tired old sun is sliding down another late-summer day. Inside the church it's cooler, and the window light is starting to fade.

As we go up to the iconostasis and stand for a moment before the icon of the Virgin (you'll find it on the front right of the color panels), we notice a few flowers laid along the wooden frame below her image. Some of these look like they're a few days old and starting to get shriveled. It doesn't look like an organized effort, not like something put on by the ladies of the flower guild. A short-stemmed dandelion has closed up tight and is going to seed.

Over the next half-hour before this summer evening service we watch many people arrive

27

and go up, it seems, to greet the Virgin. They cross themselves and may bow to touch the floor. They lean forward to kiss her on the hand and to kiss the Child's little foot; some kiss their fingertips and then press them to the icon. A couple of people leave rosebuds or daisies that they've brought from home. In front of the icon there is an elaborate brass stand which holds tiers of slim beeswax candles. Worshipers come up with candles and light them from the ones already burning, stand quietly a moment, then add them to the display.

You might be feeling uncomfortable with all this. You wouldn't be the first. You might be having two separate problems with this activity, in fact. One could be with Mary herself—how should we regard her? She should be respected, of course, but isn't all this a little too much?

The other objection may have to do with the way icons are being treated. Are these idols? It does look suspicious. If they're not idols, why do people kiss them, leave flowers, burn candles in front of them?

This question was a significant one for Christians in the early centuries. Of course, our faith grew from Judaism, which forbids the use of images. But Gentile converts far from Palestine were accustomed to Greek and Roman art and, for example, would depict on catacomb walls a Good Shepherd with a lamb on His shoulders, or a woman standing with her hands raised in prayer (called the *orans*, or "praying," position). A tradition of Christian representational painting and portraiture arose, and by the fourth century St. Basil the Great could praise artists for depicting a martyr with more eloquence than he could in words.

These paintings served as picture Bibles in an era when most people were illiterate, and when even the educated could rarely afford such an expensive hand-copied book. Since icons bore the weighty responsibility of conveying Scripture, they began to follow consistent patterns. Icons of the Crucifixion, for example, would generally present the same people at the foot of the Cross, in the same general arrangement. You wouldn't want an artist to be imaginative in depicting this scene any more than you'd want a Bible translator to apply his creativity to describing the scene in words. Icons could tell the story consistently and clearly, even where Bibles weren't available; in fact, an iconographer is sometimes said to "write" rather than "paint" an icon, since it is conveying Scripture by a different medium. As the faith spread across language and cultural barriers, portable icons were no doubt indispensable to missionaries.

However, some feared that Bible images would prove a temptation for naïve or super-stitious believers. Bishop Epiphanios of Salamis dramatically tore down a curtain that had been woven with a religious scene, as a protest against what he believed was the misuse of images. Even a thousand years later some medieval frescoes appear with their eyes scratched out—perhaps by opponents of icons, or perhaps by folk who hoped the powdered paint could cure illness.

The question of the legitimacy of Christian painting was complicated by frequent theological debates about the Incarnation of

Christ, and about matter in general. For example, the Gnostics believed that spiritual things are good and physical things are evil (a mistake that continues to confuse some Christians today). If matter is evil, they said, Jesus would not have taken on a human body. Perhaps he just projected the illusion of a body, like a hologram. And what about the wood and paint you use to make a painting? That's matter too. Better to stay away from the whole thing.

In the seventh century a military crisis brought this issue to a head. A new faith, Islam, had arisen and was sweeping over the Eastern world. Syria, Egypt, Iraq, Persia, and Jerusalem fell to Muslim conquerors, and even the imperial capital of Constantinople was attacked.

Christians were aware that both Islam and the other great Middle Eastern faith, Judaism, denounced the use of images. Some began to feel that use of religious art presented an insurmountable barrier to evangelism. Others looked at Christian cities falling to con-querors and wondered if the Jewish and

31

Muslim critique was correct. In A.D. 726, after Constantinople had suffered repeated attacks, Emperor Leo III removed the icon of Christ that stood over the Bronze Gate. This began the "iconoclast controversy" (*iconoclasm* means the smashing of icons), an often-bloody conflict that nearly split the Empire and lasted over a century.

As you look at people coming into church this evening, who stand quietly before the icon of Mary with their heads bowed, you wonder how this side was able to win. After all, the controversy was at root a conflict between church and state, with Christians resisting the Empire's attempt to tell them how they could worship. In any such conflict the state has more power, and many believers died defending the use of icons. Icons were crushed, burned, painted over, or in the case of large mosaics, covered with plaster. Most of the icons made before the eighth century were lost, with only a few in remote locations—such as the Christ of Sinai in the last chapter—surviving.

The controversy boiled down to this question: Does an image of a person have any connection to the person? Does how we treat an image "pass through" it, so to speak, to the person himself?

You might immediately think, "Of course not. That's superstition." But consider the episode a few years ago when a singer tore up a photo of the Pope on live television. Even non-Christians were appalled, and the singer was widely condemned. But one could logically say, "What does it matter? It was only paper and ink. It didn't really hurt him."

While we don't want to treat images as idols, we understand that there is some connection between an image and the person depicted, and that honor or disrespect shown to the image applies to the person. The monk known as St. Stephen the New (he was "new" in the eighth century, when he received the title to distinguish him from the St. Stephen in the book of Acts) made this point to Emperor Constantine Copronymous, son of Emperor Leo above. St. Stephen was challenged to trample on an icon of Christ, to demonstrate that the painting was a mere object with no real connection to the Lord.

33

He instead placed on the ground a coin bearing the Emperor's image and set his foot on it. St. Stephen was condemned to death.

The conflict reached a turning point in 787, when the Empress Irene convened the Seventh Ecumenical Council. At this point it wasn't possible to go back to the simple view of an icon as a useful teaching tool. The controversy had forced Christians to think through what icons were and how they should be honored.

One of the leading defenders of icons, St. John of Damascus (who, ironically, was spared persecution by the emperors because he lived in Muslim-controlled territory), stated that an icon was not an idol because it did not claim to capture God. An icon was a depiction of Christ or a saint, and as such could teach and evoke devotion. We might give a little child a picture Bible, or hang a painting of the Last Supper in our dining room, with the same intention.

Although the Old Testament forbade images, in the Incarnation God had willed to make himself visible. What He showed us in

His flesh we are free to depict. In fact, to refuse to make images of Christ is to shy away from the scandal of the Incarnation and to line up with the Gnostics, who could not accept Jesus' physical manifestation. Of course, we don't make images based on speculation about heaven or the secret things of God. That would be presumptuous and idolatrous. But we may depict those things that God has made visible to us in history. We *should* depict those things; what God has made boldly manifest we should not shyly conceal.

There should be no concern that humble earthly materials are unworthy of this use. All of creation is shot through with the presence of God. By becoming human, God reclaimed all of human nature, and all of creation was revealed as His. An icon of Christ can represent His complete human-divine unity, though it depicts His visible earthly form. It can do this using humble wood and paint, because even those ordinary things belong to Him.

Finally, how was an icon to be treated? The decision of the Council was that it should receive veneration or honor, but not worship. Worship is for God alone. Icons can be treated with respect, however, as might be expressed by bowing low before a king, or kissing the hand of a queen.

This is perhaps one of the most troubling aspects of icons for Western Christians. As you watch the flowers and candles accumulate around the icon of the Virgin tonight, you might be feeling increasingly uneasy.

When I was writing this book, I visited a cemetery and noticed the flowers on some of the graves. I imagined how a team of anthropologists from another culture might view this practice. One of them might say to the others, "The families of the dead must think their ancestors are able to smell these flowers." Another might respond, "No, they are trying to placate their ancestors by offering them gifts, so they won't come back and haunt them." A third might say, "No, these flowers confer special status on the dead in the afterlife, making them more important than those who don't have flowers."

What would you say to these anthropologists? I'd say something like, "You don't understand at all. The placing of flowers doesn't mean anything as literal as you suppose. It's a way of expressing love and honor. It's hard to explain, but if you wait and watch what people do, you'll come to understand how this little act of placing flowers fits into a larger context of beliefs."

That's how it is with venerating icons. In Eastern cultures, where kissing is a more common form of greeting and respect than for us in the West, the hands and feet of icon figures would frequently be kissed. And, just as these people would kneel and bow with forehead to the ground before a great ruler, they would "make a prostration" when the icon of the Crucifixion is carried through the church.

The Seventh Ecumenical Council stated that, "The honor paid to the icon is conveyed to its prototype." This meant that the icon is not merely a reminder of the person depicted, but can move us into contact with them—the icon is a "window into heaven," it is said. (A statue doesn't provide this connection as easily. It is captive in its setting and readily "sized up" by the viewer, while a painting appears to go on forever past its plane.) We should not stop at the surface of an icon, imagining that the wood and paint imprison deity like an idol. Rather we go through the icon, bringing our minds and hearts into the presence of the person depicted there.

The best analogy would be to the Bible. We don't think of the bundle of paper and ink as itself having special divine power; we wouldn't eat pages of a Bible to cure illness. Yet we do expect that we can go through the Bible, so to speak, and encounter God Himself. A Bible is a "window into heaven." The Council drew exactly that connection. It said that we should give to icons the kind of honor we give to the Gospels. With Bibles, we show honor by stamping "Holy Bible" on the cover, perhaps giving it a leather binding and edging the pages with gold. We treat the book with respectful care; depending on the culture in which we were raised, we might even kiss it. We would feel wounded if we saw someone tear up a Bible. But if we were accused of treating our Bibles like idols we would explain that it wasn't the physical book that we were honoring, but the God whom we meet through it. A Bible deserves respect, but not worship.

The Seventh Ecumenical Council did not permanently end the iconoclast controversy. Opponents regathered their forces, and a second wave of destruction began in 815. Another Empress, St. Theodora, paved the way for a proclamation on March 11, 843, which established a final restoration of icons. There is, naturally, an icon commemorating this moment. It shows St. Theodora and many others gathered in ranks, boldly holding up icons.

I say "final restoration of icons" but of course the debate over Christian art sporadically rose again. When Ulrich Zwingli brought the Reformation to Zurich in the early sixteenth century, one of his first acts was to smash religious statuary in the churches, a renewed iconoclast movement. But the impulse to use artistic depiction to honor people is hard to resist. I'm told that if today you visit the historic church he pastored, you'll see a statue of Zwingli outside.

That's rather a lot of history to go through, and as the light outside fades, the time for the service is drawing near. But you still may be troubled by the other question. All this may explain why people *venerate* or pray before icons of Christ, but tonight an icon of Mary is receiving all this attention. Tonight's service will be a series of intercessory prayers sung to Christ, but also to Mary. Who do we think she is?

It's been said that all icons are ultimately icons of Christ. When we look at Mary or a saint we see the power of the One who saved and transformed them, who works in history, who turns ordinary humans into saints.

And Mary is an ordinary human. Ordinary, that is, in the sense that she had normal human DNA, was born the same way we were, and like us ate and drank and slept. She's not a demi-god or mythological composite figure, part human and part divine. But she's an extraordinary human, too, in the way anyone can be who lets the light of Christ fill him or her completely.

This icon of Mary, then, tells the story of what God accomplished in her, and how He transformed her to be the bearer of His Son. She did in a literal way what we each hope to do spiritually, to be filled with Christ's presence. Often in ancient hymns she is compared to the Burning Bush, wholly on fire with the presence of God and yet unconsumed. Though the power of the Most High has overshadowed her, she is still fully herself, intact and uncompromised. Mary is set before us as a preeminent example, showing how this transformation looks in practice in one ordinary, extraordinary life.

In this icon she is shown, as usual, as a young woman holding the Christ Child. There's a reason we see her this way (and in fact icons never depict Mary by herself). Some of the early theological controversies grew from the difficulty people had in believing that Jesus was actually God from all eternity. This difficulty is by no means rare; even today we find many people who are attracted to Jesus, but can't believe He's really the eternal God. Perhaps He's just a great teacher, they say, or someone who grew up and then attained god-consciousness.

Christians have always insisted, against this view, that Jesus was God even when He was a baby. Even before He was born! We push the point by showing people pictures of Him as an infant in His mother's arms. Although we respect Abraham Lincoln a great deal, we don't go around showing baby pictures of him cuddled in his mother's arms. (It's hard to even imagine; that stovepipe hat and beard keep getting in the way.) But we use lots of baby pictures of Jesus, because we are making an urgent point about His eternal identity.

Look up at the large icon that fills the apse, behind the altar. We noticed earlier that it shows Mary standing in prayer with her hands upraised, and Jesus in a blue disk on her torso. This is more than a baby picture; it is meant to be a glimpse into her womb. The Child looks at us with regal dignity, wearing glorious robes and lifting His hand in blessing. All around Him the deep blue sky is spattered with stars. Some of the early hymns express wonder at how the Creator of the universe—in a sense, all the universe itself—could be enclosed within Mary's womb. "He made your body more spacious than the heavens," we sing.

These controversies about Jesus' divinity are why we call Mary *Theotokos*, a Greek term meaning "Birthgiver of God." It isn't precise enough to call her "the mother of God"; after all, we could call another woman "the mother of the bishop" (or of Abraham Lincoln). Jesus didn't just grow up to become God, He already was God before all eternity. Mary isn't the mother of His humanity alone; she is Theotokos, because the child she bore was God Himself. It's been said that the term "Theotokos" contains in a single world the entire theology of Christ's person.

If this were merely about theological concepts, however, we wouldn't be seeing the church fill with people ending a long workday with a visit to church. They love Mary. Look again at this image of her on the iconostasis. Look at her wide, dark eyes. These worshipers are gathering to pray to her, or rather, to ask her to pray for them.

43

Mary is present on the iconostasis in her role as an intercessor. You may have known some great "prayer warriors," people whom you'd go to first if you had a serious prayer need. Mary is the leader of all praying Christians. It might be startling to think about, but she isn't really dead. No one in Christ is dead. They have "departed," we may say; they have "fallen asleep in the Lord," and we don't plan to see them anymore on this earth. But "in the nearer presence of God" they are more alive than we are, standing in worship around the heavenly throne.

Yet these fellow believers are somehow with us, too; as the author of the Book of Hebrews says, "We are surrounded by so great a cloud of witnesses" (12:1). Both in the heavenly throne room and beside us in the Body of Christ, their whole work is to pray. We can ask them to pray for us, just as we'd ask a friend. They *are* our friends. A wall full of icons is like a scrapbook full of photos of people we love, people who love us. When we go to worship we can see how many brothers and sisters Christ has given us for our support and encouragement. We see some of them praying beside us in the flesh, and past them we see others praying in icons. They are all our friends in the Body of Christ, which transcends all time and space.

(A word on terminology: when we ask an earthly friend to pray for us, we telephone or send an e-mail; when we ask a heavenly friend to pray, we "pray" to them. The term "pray" originally meant simply to make a request, and could apply to citizens of earth or heaven. You might have said to a friend, "I pray you, remember me in your prayers." That is what these worshipers are doing; they are praying to Mary, asking her to pray for them.)

Mary, whom Jesus loved like a child loves his mother, is an especially wise and dear Christian friend. We don't preach about her to outsiders; if you were bringing someone to faith in Christ, you wouldn't start with Mary. But once you know Jesus as your Lord, you get to meet His mother, too. Just as might happen in an earthly friendship, you find that His mother is a person you're glad to know. From the Cross Jesus entrusted Mary to His friend John saying, "Behold your mother" (John 19:27). Jesus shares her with us, and it feels like she is our mother too.

She died in August. This is a solemn time of year for Orthodox Christians, as we prepare during the first two weeks of the month for her *Dormition* ("Falling-Asleep") on August 15. The icon for that day shows all the apostles in tears, gathered around Mary's still body. In their midst, unseen, Jesus stands holding in His arms a tiny swaddled figure, the soul of His mother.

At Holy Resurrection Church the community gathers for a prayer service every night these first two weeks of August. (By the way, not all Orthodox churches offer this service; parishes vary somewhat in their observances throughout the year. In this book we'll be joining Holy Resurrection Church in their particular cycle of worship.) The long intercessory hymn the church uses on these nights is called the "Paraklesis"; it asks Mary to pray for us because of our troubles and illnesses, and our tendency to fall regularly into sin. We ask for healing, and also to be given hearts that really care about becoming holy as God is holy. We ask for the gift of repentance. On the cover of my copy of the Paraklesis service is written, "To be chanted in every tribulation and in sorrow of soul."

This icon of the Theotokos on the iconostasis is eloquently expressive of tribulation and sorrow of soul. Contemporary images of Bible figures don't usually look this serious; in a Christian bookstore, the plaques and framed pictures show Christ and other Bible figures looking happy and self-assured. That's the modern-day face, the face you put on when someone takes your picture.

But this sorrowful Theotokos has a true face, too, and there must be many a person over the centuries who prayed before this icon with a sad or fearful mind. If this icon were a mirror, and we could see in it all the faces that have prayed before it, we would see so many in deep sorrow: a weeping woman whose baby had died; a man wracked with anxiety over drought-stricken fields; a family whose home lay in the path of an approaching army. Each stood here with a face that mirrored the Theotokos' own deep sorrow, then

47

turned to bear whatever challenges lay ahead. Swift time laid their bodies in the dust, and all their sorrows, once so monumental, have been forgotten by every living soul. But I think the Theotokos remembers. Somehow, I think this Theotokos remembers all the faces she has seen.

Unlike the Christ of Sinai, which comes out toward you, this icon pulls you in with the force of gravity. The original of this image, it is said, was painted by St. Luke (some say this is a copy of Luke's painting, and others that this *is* Luke's painting). It seems that Luke knew Mary; his Gospel recounts details that other evangelists do not include and personal notes which could have come only from her. Alone among the Evangelists, Luke describes how the angel Gabriel came to her to announce Christ's conception, and how she felt about the events of His birth and child-hood ("Mary kept all these things, pondering them in her heart" [Luke 2:19]). He tells the story from Mary's point of view.

Whenever this icon was painted, it is first noted in history in Kiev about 1132, after which it spent a couple of centuries in Vladimir before finding a permanent home in Moscow in 1395. It is still called the Virgin of Vladimir and is perhaps Russia's most beloved icon. In times of danger it has been taken into the streets of the city with fervent prayers for protection, even as recently as 1993. It is associated with many miraculous deliverances from Tartar attack throughout the fourteenth through sixteenth centuries. The men who turned back foreign invaders in 1612 declared, "It is better for us to die than to deliver the image of the immaculate Mother of God of Vladimir to desecration."

This icon is the finest example of a type called the Virgin of Tenderness, which shows the Christ Child pressing His face to His mother's cheek. Sometimes instead the Child is sitting upright in her arms, and Mary gestures toward Him as if presenting her child to us; this kind is called "Directress." The large icon we see in the apse, where Christ appears as a child in her womb, is called the Virgin of the Sign, as in Isaiah's prophecy, "The Lord shall give you a sign: Behold, a virgin shall conceive and bear a son" (Isa. 7:14 RSV alternative).

If you look more closely at the Virgin of Vladimir you can see that it has been repainted many times. Even in this reproduction you can see changing patterns in the Child's garment, and in the original they create a broken, multilayered surface texture. Yet the deeply expressive faces, and the Child's little hand around His mother's neck, are original. They shine through the centuries: the steady, receptive gaze of the Virgin, and the bright cup of the Child's face turned up toward hers.

As with the Christ of Sinai, this icon tells a two-part story. Our initial impression is of the Virgin's dark eyes, which draw us in. Her figure makes a large dark triangle, like a stormy wave, against the red-golden background. On this darkness the only light is her golden hand banded with red. Perhaps it is gesturing toward her son; perhaps it is falling downwards, opening in submission, calling us into the ocean of her great sorrow.

It makes me think of the Scripture: "Is it nothing to you, all you who pass by? Look and see if there is any sorrow like my sorrow which was brought upon me" (Lam. 1:12).

Look and see. There is sorrow like hers around us all the time, perhaps even in the life of the hand that holds this book. Inevitably, most other people pass by a grieving person as if it is nothing to them, perhaps because they are huddled over their own secret sorrows.

The Virgin's dark, direct gaze pierces the isolation that walls us up, separate and alone. Whatever we are, we are not alone. Whatever will happen, we will not go through it alone. Her eyes do not promise that what is going to happen will be easy. She looks into a future where her beloved son will die. But nothing in her regal bearing rejects this coming pain. In her steady resolve we, too, find strength to bear whatever will come.

What became of all the people who prayed fervently before this icon? Some asked for healing, deliverance, peace, and some received what they asked for. Others did not. All eventually lost everything. That is God's expectation: One day we will lose everything, body, life, health, possessions, position, parents, spouse, and child. All that we fret over losing by increments now, we will lose absolutely and completely one day. All flesh must come to dust. Everyone must lose everything.

But some who lose all "will receive a hundredfold, and inherit eternal life" (Matt. 19:29). "For all things are yours, whether . . . the world or life or death or the present or the future, all are yours; and you are Christ's; and Christ is God's" (1 Cor. 3:21–23).

Christ looks up at His mother, and His bright round face is lit with joy. It is not that He is ignorant of what lies ahead; the reverse is true. He sees farther ahead than His mother does, to a victory no human could imagine. He sees complete victory, when all creation is restored, when justice is fully done and all tears are wiped away. No sorrow, great or secret, is forgotten by God. All will be made right some day. The generations who in centuries past prayed in fear or longing before this icon lost everything in death, then gained everything in eternal life, because they are Christ's and Christ's is God's. They have passed through to the other side of this window.

We stand on this side preoccupied, confused, and sorrowful. We come each night in the first two weeks of August, preparing for the loss of this dear mother Christ has given us. We pray before her icon, leave flowers, light candles, and sing hymns, turning now to the Lord in prayers for deliverance, and now to the Theotokos, asking her to pray for us. She is listening closely.

From The Dormition Paraklesis

To God's birthgiver let us run now most earnestly,
we sinners all and wretched ones,
and fall prostrate in repentance
calling from the depth of our souls:
Lady, come unto our aid,
have compassion upon us;
hasten, for we are lost in a throng of
    transgressions.

Entreaty do I pour forth unto the Lord,
and to Him do I proclaim all my sorrows,
for many woes fill my soul to repletion,
and lo, my life unto Hades has now drawn nigh.
Like Jonah do I pray to You,
raise me up from corruption, O Lord my God.

Sorrow has fettered me, and I am unable
to endure and bear the demon's darts;
a shelter have I none, nor a place to run,
I the wretched one.
Embattled from all sides am I,
and no consolation have I but you.

From you is no one turned away ashamed
  and empty
who runs to you for refuge, O pure Virgin
  Theotokos.

You are the sweetness of angels, the gladness
  of afflicted ones,
and the protectress of Christians, O Virgin
Mother of our Lord;
be my helper and save me
from out of eternal torments.

You art a gold entwined tower and twelve
  wall encircled city,
a throne besprinkled with sunbeams, a royal
  chair of the king;
O inexplicable wonder, that you milkfeed
  the Master!

O you Apostles from afar,
being now gathered together here in the
  town of Gethsemane,
give burial to my body, give burial to my body,
and You, my Son and God,
receive my spirit.

CHAPTER THREE

The Resurrection

It looks like some kind of crazy party has been going on in here. It's four o'clock in the morning, and the floor of the church is covered with leaves—fresh bay leaves, it turns out, which yield a pungent fragrance as they're pressed underfoot. The leaves are spotted with candle drippings, and stubs of candles and little paper candle-bibs are everywhere. The chairs that line the church walls are askew. The Oriental rug that fills the main body of the church is marked by encampments of throw pillows and baby blankets where children dozed off during the four-hour service. The choir music stands are mounded with twice the usual number of books, and the choir director's bedroom slippers lie toe-crossed on the podium. Rosewater, generously hurled around earlier, has left streaks in the faint soot of the upper walls. All that's missing is confetti.

Downstairs there's a roar of the party continuing, as parishioners drink champagne, eat ham and cheese, and share chocolates from large baskets covered with embroidered cloths. As they left the church the priest gave each one a hardboiled egg with a red shell. Now people pair up to knock these together until only one egg in the room is left triumphantly uncrunched. Lent is over! Pascha has come! Schoolchildren on the first day of summer are hardly this exuberant.

Upstairs it's relatively quiet. Banks of lilies spill out below the iconostasis, and above it each icon is topped with an orchid, like mistletoe inviting a kiss. But the icon most celebrated today, the special guest at the party, is the complicated-looking one on the far left (and on the front left of the color panels), where Jesus stands on two crossed white planks.

He fills the entire center of the icon, and all eyes are on Him; Jesus is the firm center of this story. His white robe billows up behind

Him like smoke, and a shimmering blue disk suggests a halo of light emanating from His entire body (called a *mandorla*). Jesus looks solid and muscular, and everything about Him conveys energy and decisive action. This place is Hades, the realm and region of Death, and unconquerable light has just broken in.

Jesus is reaching down to drag Adam from his boxlike stone tomb, grasping Him firmly by the wrist—by the wrist, not the hand. All the energy flows from Jesus. Adam is a smaller, bent figure, an old man—*the* Old Man—and he is dragged up out of death by a power not his own. He lifts his right hand toward Jesus in a gesture of surprise and thanksgiving. On the right Eve is rising as well, clothed in brilliant red. In some variations of this icon (this example is from sixteenth-century Russia), Jesus is holding Adam's wrist in one hand and Eve's in the other, while looking directly out at us. You're next!

Behind Adam are others of the righteous dead, prophets and forerunners. White-haired King David is standing in the front line with his youthful, dark-haired son King Solomon. Solomon might be saying to his dad, "What did I tell you?" Both of them stretch their arms toward Jesus in astonishment and appeal. Beyond Solomon we see John the Baptist, now recapitated, with his characteristic tousled hair still in place. He has not been waiting as long as David and Solomon, and modestly stands in the background. Yet his attention is fixed on Jesus, and his unconsciously imploring open hand echoes his appearance in the icon beside the Christ of Sinai on the other end of the iconostasis. More retiring still is the figure dimly visible between David and Solomon, who is wearing a small, round hat with a red top. This is the prophet Daniel, and he can't have a very good view of Jesus, with David's and Solomon's haloes getting in the way.

The prophets of ancient Israel are included in this image as heralds and ancestors of Christ. Like us, they are justified by faith, as the ancient hymn (called a *troparion*) says:

You have justified the Forefathers by faith,
  and through them
You have gone before and betrothed to
Yourself a Church from among the nations.
The Saints boast in glory that from their
  seed there is glorious fruit,
which is she who gave birth to You without
  seed.
Wherefore, by their prayers, O Christ God,
save our souls.

High above the scene the blue-tipped mountains reel and dance. Two angels hold a Cross and chalice, emblems of how the victory was won, the victory being celebrated with bay leaves, rosewater, and feasting till dawn on this spring morning.

And this brings us to the black pit under Jesus' feet. Sooner or later we have to ask, what was this a victory over?

This icon is known as the *Anastasis*, meaning Resurrection. It's not the image we associate with the Resurrection in Western art; there we picture the garden tomb and the stone rolled away, Jesus rising in white garments, his hand lifted in greeting. For Western Christians the events of Easter weekend are bookended with the Crucifixion on one end and the empty tomb on the other. The time in the middle is hidden, silent as a tomb.

For Christians of the icon tradition, however, this time-between-times has momentous importance. It is when He "went and preached to the spirits in prison" (1 Pet. 3:19) and "led a host of captives" (Eph. 4:8). This hidden Saturday concerns the Resurrection, not only of Christ but of everybody.

With this our understanding of Christ's work is expanded. It is more than just the events of a Friday afternoon; it begins with the plan made before the foundation of the world, the Son's decision to become incarnate for our salvation. In the second chapter of the letter to the Philippians we find this, the earliest existing Christian hymn:

> Who, though He was in the form of God, did not count equality with God a thing to be grasped, but emptied himself, taking the form of a servant. . . . (2:6-7)

This was the sacrifice Jesus offered to His Father: He agreed to empty himself and become human. This was not a reluctant obedience, of course. We could imagine a brave soldier and his general conferring on the best way of making a daring rescue. The soldier volunteers for the risky mission, even though he knows it will cost his life. It is a sacrifice offered in love to the general, yet fully expresses the soldier's will as well.

The Philippians hymn continues:

And being found in human form He humbled himself and became obedient unto death, even death on a cross. (2:8)

At the top of the icon angels stand with the Cross; at the bottom, Jesus stands on crossed planks of wood, a broken door. These are the gates of Hades, which He has knocked down and demolished. It took becoming human for Him to be able to die; it took death to get Him into the realm of Death. But that's where we were, held captive due to our sins. That's where He had to go, in order to set us free.

It's tempting to think of this as a nice thing Jesus did a long time ago; it's hard to realize how much we need it. That is the challenge of this icon. In the previous chapters we looked deeply into the eyes of Christ and the Theotokos, and encountered something that moves us. But when we look at this scene we seem to be looking at a picture from a fantastic book of ancient history. How does it relate to us today?

The problem, at root, is that we don't identify with Adam and Eve, trapped in their tombs. Frankly, we find it hard to believe that we are sinners. It's not that sinners don't exist; we just don't think we fit the category. Our culture would readily point fingers at the sin evidenced by bad guys like racists, sexists, polluters, and rich people. We reflexively think of ourselves on the good-guy side, fighting against all that. If we're on the good side, then Jesus already likes us, and we don't really need salvation. Nice of Him to do it, though, like getting a sweater for Christmas from your aunt.

That's why we have trouble locating ourselves in this icon. We've fallen into that most omnipresent of spiritual traps, complacent self-righteousness. We feel comfortable locating sin out there, in those deplorable bad guys, but don't recognize it in ourselves. This may sound like a negligible failing, but it is the single greatest barrier to spiritual progress. Jesus' warnings against self-righteousness are frequent, from the exhortation to remove the plank in your own eye rather than the mote in your brother's, to the reminder that He came to call sinners, not the righteous. He wouldn't have brought it up so often if it weren't an ever-present temptation. Until we're willing to see ourselves standing helpless beside Adam and Eve, yearning for rescue, we won't understand this icon. We won't understand salvation.

But how does the imagery of imprisonment fit in? If anything, we may ruefully say the problem is that we're too free; we do things impulsively that hurt others and ourselves, and set us all tumbling through space. A little more constraint sounds like a blessing. How is our sin, wrought in acts of exuberant

64

self-will, like its seeming opposite: being held prisoner, locked in a tomb?

At night after I turn out the light, sometimes I think about all the people who are suffering at that moment. I have been worrying about car trouble or computer trouble, but somewhere in my city today someone learned that he is dying. Someone today heard the words, "I don't love you any more." Someone is thinking, "I'm getting old. I will never be loved." Some elderly person heard a son or daughter scream, "Why don't you just die!" A child's mother, or a mother's child, has just died, and when the survivor is all alone this first night she can't stop crying. There are many people suffering, all alone, all together, under the dark wing of this night.

But even worse to think of, someone is being held captive. A woman is being raped again and again, and doesn't know if in the morning she will be free or dead. A young man has been captured by enemy soldiers, and they are amusing themselves by keeping him alive, a bloody toy, as long as possible. While you were flipping around the channels, frustrated that there was nothing good on TV, a child was undergoing something horrible in his own home, probably because mommy has a new boyfriend. When you read about it in the paper a month from now, you will drop your face into your hands and weep.

That is what it means to be held captive, under the power of someone else, someone who hates and wants to hurt you. And we are captives: "Everyone who commits sin is a slave to sin," Jesus said. In a bitter paradox, our self-willed exercise of freedom, our defiant assertion of power and choice, enslaves us. Every choice outside the will of God is like choosing to live without oxygen. He is light and life, and striking out in another direction is death. Even worse, it is enslavement, as Jesus said; it is coming under the power of another, who wants to hurt us.

Jesus' victory was targeted. It was a victory *over* someone, the "Evil One" whom He, in the Lord's Prayer, instructs us to pray to be delivered from. It turns out that God and humans aren't the only forces in the universe. If that's the case, sin isn't just a private affair, a matter of goofing up in an excusable, only-human way. It is holding out your wrists and asking to be manacled. It will confine you here, in this icon, entombed in a pit.

The sin in our hearts, which seems so insignificant, is just one tributary of a dark river uniting us spiritually with those who torture, hate, and kill. We are amateurs, dabbling in backbiting and gossip perhaps, showing off, telling weasely lies. We're like the sidekicks in a movie, who tail after the big boss and yell, "You get 'em!" in our pipsqueak voices. We do our part to help his cause, by being sullen or envious, and by thinking up zingers that will humiliate someone we dislike.

We are captives. Our minds are captive. We love evil rather than good, darkness rather than light (John 3:19). We have the illusion that we are nice people, and do not know that we are lost, vulnerable, imprisoned, captives of the Evil that hates all human life. Jesus says to us, as He did to the lukewarm church at Laodicea, "You say, I am rich, I have prospered, and I need nothing; not knowing that you are wretched, pitiable, poor, blind, and naked" (Rev. 3:17).

We are pitiable. Our true condition is shown by the impenetrable blackness filling Adam's and Eve's tombs; from the side these look like shallow boxes, but from the top we see that they have no bottom. They empty into the bleak pit that goes on forever, dark and starred with metal bits, keys and locks and tools that hint of torture.

Jesus takes pity on us. This is why we call Him "Savior." He saves us, literally, from a fate worse than death, a situation we waltzed into willingly, and couldn't escape to save our lives. Jesus hauls crouching Adam up by the wrist, and all he can do is be grateful. The more we realize what we have been rescued from, the more grateful we are; the deeper we see into the pit, the higher we glimpse the peaks of God's love.

One day a year is set aside particularly to revel in this victory, and it's no wonder worshipers celebrate all night long. A few hours ago they heard a short sermon, one which set the tone for their exuberant mood. It is the same Easter sermon they heard last year, and every year before that; it is the same sermon Orthodox Christians have heard every Pascha since the fifth century. Nobody ever gets tired of it. It was written by St. John Chrysostom, the bishop of Constantinople who was known for his vigorous eloquence.

St. John begins his brisk sermon, reproduced below in entirety, by recalling Jesus' parable of the workers in the vineyard (Matt. 20:1-16). St. John addresses the fear that follows the first stirring of spiritual awakening: Could this invitation include even me? Have I fallen too far down the pit for Jesus to reach me? Am I too late?

The Paschal Sermon of St. John Chrysostom

If any man be devout and love God, let him enjoy this fair and radiant triumphal feast.
If any man be a wise servant, let him enter rejoicing into the joy of his Lord.

If any have labored long in fasting,
let him now receive his recompense.
If any have wrought from the first hour,
let him today receive his just reward.
If any have come at the third hour,
let him with thankfulness keep the feast.
If any have arrived at the sixth hour,
let him have no misgivings, because he shall
in no wise be deprived.
If any have delayed until the ninth hour,
let him draw near, fearing nothing.
If any have tarried even until the eleventh hour,
let him also be not alarmed at his tardiness;
for the Lord, who is jealous of His honor,
will accept the last even as the first;
He gives rest unto him who comes at the
eleventh hour, even as unto him who has
worked from the first hour.
And He shows mercy upon the last, and
cares for the first; and to the one He gives,
and upon the other He bestows gifts.
And He both accepts the deeds, and welcomes
the intention, and honors the acts and
praises the offering.

Wherefore, enter all of you into the joy of
  your Lord, and receive your reward,
both the first and likewise the second.
You rich and poor together, hold high festival.
You sober and you heedless, honor the day.
Rejoice today, both you who have fasted and
  you who have disregarded the fast.
The table is fully laden; feast sumptuously.
The calf is fatted; let no one go hungry away.
Enjoy the feast of faith; receive all the riches
  of loving-kindness.
Let no one bewail his poverty,
for the universal kingdom has been revealed.
Let no one weep for his iniquities,
for pardon has shone forth from the grave.
Let no one fear death, for the Savior's death
  has set us free:
He that was held prisoner of it has
  annihilated it.

By descending into hell, He made hell captive.
He embittered it when it tasted of His flesh.
And Isaiah, foretelling this, cried:
"Hell was embittered when it encountered
  You in the lower regions."

71

It was embittered, for it was abolished.
It was embittered, for it was mocked.
It was embittered, for it was slain.
It was embittered, for it was overthrown.
It was embittered, for it was fettered in chains.
It took a body, and met God face to face.
It took earth, and encountered heaven.
It took that which was seen, and fell upon
  the unseen.

O Death, where is your sting?
O Hell, where is your victory?
Christ is risen, and you are overthrown.
Christ is risen, and the demons are fallen.
Christ is risen, and the angels rejoice.
Christ is risen, and life reigns.
Christ is risen, and not one dead remains in
  the grave.
For Christ, being risen from the dead,
is become the first-fruits of those who have
  fallen asleep.
To Him be glory and dominion unto ages of
ages. Amen.

CHAPTER FOUR

St. John the Baptist

This time we've come to the church on an ordinary day when no service is scheduled, an afternoon just before Labor Day. It's the time of year for Back-to-School, and long after we finish school for good we still associate this season with fresh beginnings. In the old Roman Empire this was the New Year; September 1 inaugurated a new cycle at the optimistic time of harvests, and the Christian calendar followed the same observance. The old year is running out, and we have come to the final feast of the liturgical cycle, the commemoration of St. John the Baptist.

August 29 is, in fact, one of several days dedicated to St. John in the yearly cycle. This one honors his death, and it is one of the rare feast days that is also a day of strict fast. Because St. John was beheaded, some Slavic Christians add further restrictions to their fast: no platters, no knives, no food that is red or spherical.

In Orthodox churches St. John is often called "the Forerunner" rather than "the Baptist"; his full title is "the Holy and Glorious Prophet, Forerunner, and Baptist John." He doesn't look very glorious in this icon, on the far right of the iconostasis (and the back right of the color panels), but rather contemplative and tender. Though usually the origins of icons are unknown, we know that this one was made by a gifted iconographer named Euphrosynos, a native of Crete. Euphrosynos was a monk at Holy Dionysiou Monastery on Mt. Athos, which is a peninsula off the Greek coast that has been a preeminent center of Orthodox spirituality for centuries. Its rugged slopes today house about twenty main monasteries and many other hermitages and *sketes* (small communities). In 1542 Euphrosynos executed a series of icons for the monastery, including this one of St. John standing, turned toward his Lord in prayer. An arrangement with Jesus in the middle and a line of supplicating figures reaching to each side is called a *deisis*.

This isn't the only way St. John might appear. Sometimes he faces us, perhaps holding a scroll reading "Repent, for the kingdom of heaven is at hand" (Matt. 3:2). He may carry a thin staff that terminates in a cross, while raising his right hand in blessing. He may also be shown holding a platter containing his severed head, or standing in a rocky landscape with such a dish at his feet. Nearby there may be a stunted tree, split by an axe. St. John said, "Even now the axe is laid to the root of the trees; every tree therefore that does not bear good fruit is cut down and thrown into the fire" (Matt. 3:10).

Besides all this, St. John is sometimes shown with voluminous red or rainbow-colored wings, signifying his title "Angel of the Desert." Always imposing, St. John usually looks serious or even sad, and if turned toward the Lord his head is distinctly bowed. His appearance is disheveled, as befits a desert-dweller, and under his cloak he usually (though not here) wears a furry tunic of long camel hair.

You might wonder, what has he got to be so repentant about? St. John was no dissolute, but led an ascetic life in the wilderness. According to tradition, Herod's slaughter of the Innocents spread to include John's father, the priest Zechariah, who was murdered in the temple. John's mother, Elizabeth, fled with him to the wilderness, where he was raised by angels. Mark has barely begun his Gospel when he bluntly announces, "John the baptizer appeared in the wilderness," kicking things off with a jolt. St. John simply appears and immediately begins to deliver his insistent, unvarying message: Repent.

In this icon, however, he is looking at his Lord, not us. His face is softened and combines beseeching intercession with tranquil gratitude. These two elements must always be kept in balance: We must always ask for mercy, but never need to be anxious about receiving it; we can always be confident of God's love, but must never take it for granted. As St. John stands, turned toward his Lord in prayer, we stand likewise beside St. John, learning how to pray.

In fact, this is a hard icon to focus on, because it doesn't want to hold our gaze. St. John's hands keep scooping our attention back over to that commanding icon of Christ, from whom everything on the iconostasis radiates. "He must increase, and I must decrease," St. John said. I can imagine him saying to his iconographer, "Why are you making an icon of me? Look over there—see where I'm pointing? That's what's important!"

We might please St. John best, then, if we allow him to escape our scrutiny and merge back into the larger community of saints. There he is, in the background of the Resurrection icon, standing behind King Solomon, with his whole attention fixed on Christ. Was it Herod's will to behead him? Or Herodias's, or Salome's? Underlying all this was the providential will of God, who sent his messenger before his face, even into the depths of Hades. There, too, St. John would proclaim, "Prepare the way of the Lord." Even there the rough places would be made smooth, and light flood into every dark corner.

We stand next to St. John with our hands raised in prayer, learning to balance supplication and gratitude, like learning to ride a two-wheeled bike. Even in an empty church we are two or three gathered together, and in a mystery represent the entire Body of Christ. Even when alone we are not alone.

A friend of mine, a priest, once served vespers with only a handful of people in the congregation, including his elderly father who was quite ill with Alzheimer's disease. During the service the priest began to notice something. The singing sounded unusually beautiful, rich and full and sincere. It sounded like a great many voices, though he could see only a few people standing in the little church. Yet whenever they began to sing an entire heavenly choir burst forth.

Still wondering what had happened, he doused the lights and prepared to lock up the church. On the way out the old man said heartily, "Boy, you really packed them in there tonight!"

Startling as it sounds, this kind of story is not uncommon. People have told me of coming into an empty church and seeing a robed figure that stood in prayer in front of the icons, then suddenly vanished. My own husband, a priest, figured in a similar story. A visiting couple had lunch with us after church one Sunday, and their three-year-old daughter was seated across the table from him. Suddenly she pointed and said to her mother, "That's the man who was up there singing with the angels!"

We are less alone than we know. This can be good news or bad news, depending on how you feel about your life receiving close inspection. It's receiving close inspection whether you like it or not, of course, and one day all the books will be opened and every secret known. This can be a very disconcerting thought at first, but the more you struggle and pray to lead the best life you can, the more this help can be a relief and blessing.

What does it mean to "lead the best life you can"? Our standards for ourselves are usually pretty low; we may think, "I'm already a Christian, Jesus always forgives me, why worry about it?" But life in Christ is meant to be transforming. It's not just being "like" Christ but being "in" Christ, so that He floods every dark corner with light—corners He already knows all about, better than we do. We don't merely hope to muddle through till we die, then rocket upstairs where everything will be peachy. With that kind of attitude, you may not even endure all the way to the end, but give up when things get tough or strong temptations come along. In Jesus' parable, the sower tossed seed onto four different kinds of ground, but only one bore fruit. Yet what that seed produced was more than earthly agriculture could imagine, a hundredfold return that endures to eternity.

We can be more in Christ than we can be on our own. We can be not just nice people, but saints. Our modest aim is to get up on the iconostasis, too, to move from standing next to St. John on the carpet, to standing next to him in wood and paint. We are already part of that "great cloud of witnesses," though perhaps a fallible and uneven part; when my husband is "up there singing with the angels," I don't expect that his is the most polished voice. Bit by bit we can become what we are created to be, if we stay humble and pray for help to get there.

There's an old sermon illustration about the little girl whose pastor asked her, "What is a saint?" She thought about the stained-glass windows in her church and said, "A saint is somebody whom the light shines through."

There's something I particularly like about that analogy; it's that the brighter the light becomes, the more different the windows look from one another. At dusk, you can tell that the windows show a row of saints, but you can't tell who's who. When the light is at its brightest, every detail stands out distinctly.

It's like that with saints; the more they are filled with light, the more different they are from one another. One of the stories from the *Desert Fathers*, those prayer warriors of the early centuries, concerns two monks who made a trip to visit some of the luminaries of that age. First they decided to see the famed ascetic Abba Arsenius. He had been a wealthy senator in Rome and had a reputation for profound humility, sobriety, and penitence. (It is said that noble, silver-haired Arsenius was very handsome, except that he had wept in repentance so long that his eyelashes washed away.) The two monks traveled a long way to get to his rustic cell, and when they arrived the great man greeted their intrusion cordially but without excess conversation. The monks sat with him in silence for a while, then started feeling uncomfortable and took their leave.

Next they decided to see another giant of the desert, the former gang leader, Abba Moses. This large, physically powerful man had been a robber and murderer before coming to Christ. "When they arrived the Abba welcomed them joyfully," a very different reception than they'd had from Arsenius.

When the travelers returned to their monastery and told about their journey, a fellow monk who heard the story was puzzled. "He prayed to God saying, 'Lord, explain this matter to me. For Thy name's sake the one flees from men, and the other, for Thy name's sake, receives them with open arms.'" This prayer was answered by a vision. "Then two large boats were shown to Him on a river, and he saw Abba Arsenius and the Spirit of God sailing in one, in perfect peace; and in the other was Abba Moses with the angels of God, and they were all eating honey cakes."[1]

What variety God shows, in all the details of creation! He made each human as unique as each snowflake. In a paradox, we are all bear His image, we are all being restored to His likeness; yet when that process is complete and we all "look like" Him, we will be even more delightfully different from one another than we are now. God made only one St. John the Baptist, and He only made one of you, in the whole history of the world. The more the light shines through you, the more different you will be from the saint standing next to you. "And we all, with unveiled face, beholding the glory of the Lord, are being changed into His likeness from one degree of glory to another" (2 Cor. 3:18). Our callings and courses in life will be different; our expressions of the light in us will be unique; our final destiny will be one, when at last we're up there, singing with the angels.

[1]From Benedicta Ward, *The Sayings of the Desert Fathers* (Kalamazoo, MI: Cistercian Publications, 1987) pp.17–18.

83

By faith Abel offered to God a more acceptable sacrifice . . ., through which he received approval as righteous, God bearing witness by accepting his gifts.

By faith Enoch was taken up so that he should not see death; and he was not found, because God had taken him.

By faith Noah, being warned by God concerning events as yet unseen, took heed and constructed an ark . . .; by this . . . he became an heir of righteousness.

By faith Abraham obeyed when he was called to go out to a place which he was to receive as an inheritance; and he went out, not knowing where he was to go.

By faith Sarah herself received power to conceive, even when she was past the age, since she considered Him faithful who had promised.

By faith Jacob, when dying, blessed each of the sons of Joseph, bowing in worship over the head of his staff.

By faith Joseph, at the end of his life, made mention of the exodus of the Israelites.

By faith Moses, when he was born, was hid for three months by his parents, because they saw that the child was beautiful; and they were not afraid of the king's edict.

By faith Moses, when he was grown up, refused to be called the son of Pharaoh's daughter, choosing rather to share ill-treatment with the people of God.

By faith the people crossed the Red Sea as if on dry land.

By faith the walls of Jericho fell down after they had been encircled for seven days.

By faith Rahab the harlot did not perish . . . , because she had given friendly welcome to the spies.

And what more shall I say? For time would fail me to tell of Gideon, Barak, Samson, Jephthah, of David and Samuel and the prophets—who through faith conquered kingdoms, enforced justice, received promises, stopped the mouths of lions, quenched raging fire, escaped the edge of the sword, won strength out of weakness, became mighty in war, put foreign armies to flight. Women received their dead by resurrection.

Some were tortured, refusing to accept release, that they might rise again to a better life. Others suffered mocking and scourging, and even chains and imprisonment. They were stoned, they were sawn in two, they were killed with the sword; they went about in skins of sheep and goats, destitute, afflicted, ill-treated—of whom the world was not worthy—wandering over deserts and mountains, and in dens and caves of the earth.

And all these, though well attested by their faith, did not receive what was promised, since God had foreseen something better for us, that apart from us they should not be made perfect.

Therefore, since we are surrounded by so great a cloud of witnesses, let us also lay aside every weight, and sin which clings so closely, and let us run with perseverance the race that is set before us, looking to Jesus the pioneer and perfecter of our faith.

3. The Christ of Sinai
CHAPTER ONE

2. The Virgin of Vladimir
CHAPTER TWO

1. The Resurrection
CHAPTER THREE

4. St. John the Baptist
CHAPTER FOUR

1. The Angel with the Golden Hair
CHAPTER FIVE

2. The Annunciation
CHAPTER SIX

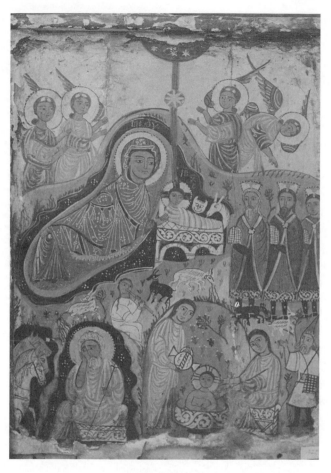

3. The Nativity
CHAPTER SEVEN

4. The Theophany
CHAPTER EIGHT

5. The Transfiguration
CHAPTER NINE

6. The Crucifixion
CHAPTER TEN

7. The Epitaphios
CHAPTER ELEVEN

8. The Old Testament Trinity
CHAPTER TWELVE

PART II

Icons of
Feasts and Saints

CHAPTER FIVE

The Angel with the Golden Hair

In our last visit to Holy Resurrection Church we looked at the icon of St. John the Baptist on the iconostasis. Though there are many more icons on the iconostasis, now we'll turn our attention elsewhere in the church. There are so many icons, on so many surfaces, that it's hard to focus on individual examples. Some depict scenes from the Bible and Church history, and some represent saints. At first these figures look generally alike, but soon you notice basic differences: The ones wearing crowns must be royalty, and ones wearing vestments must be clergy. Most are dressed in the style of their time, but some, like St. Mary of Egypt, are in rags. The widow St. Xenia of Petersburg wears her husband's military coat. Everyone has a story. Someone holding a book is likely to have been a writer, which is an encouraging sight to us writers. A doctor holds a box of medicines, a martyr holds the instrument of her death, and St. Stylianos, who took care of children, holds a swaddled baby. Someone holding a scroll may have said one extraordinarily memorable thing in his life. It makes you wonder, if they made an icon of you holding a scroll, what would it say?

Angels aren't the first thing you notice when you walk into a church full of icons. Images of Christ and the Theotokos, of other people and scenes, capture your attention first. Then you begin to realize that angels are everywhere. They're in the background of many icons, and sometimes have icons of their own. Up in the apse two angels swinging incense burners stand on either side of the Virgin of the Sign. Two more are standing guard on the *Angel Doors* of the iconostasis. Others appear in the sky or background of icons of the Crucifixion, the Resurrection, and many more. For something seen so rarely, angels are depicted with enthusiastic frequency. In a Saxon church in Bradford-on-Avon, possibly dating to the seventh century, the only surviving piece of ancient decoration is a pair of stone-carved flying angels. Angels don't often appear in visible form, but when they do they make a big impression.

November 8 is the feast of the Archangel Michael and "all the Bodiless Hosts." Michael is hailed as the "Chief Commander" of the angels, and in his icons he often appears as a military figure, in armor and carrying a sword or spear. Wherever Michael appears in Scripture—in Daniel, Jude, and John's Revelation—he is associated with combat. He is on the left door of the iconostasis.

The other chief angel, Gabriel, is on the right door. Gabriel brings messages and describes future events, for example telling Mary that she will conceive a child. In accord with his role as communicator (*angelos* means "messenger"), Gabriel has a compassionate and tender expression. These two often appear in church as a pair, and may look alike except for Michael's breastplate. They may be holding luminous globes of light, which represent the presence of Christ.

Angels are shown with smooth, youthful faces and wavy, flowing hair pulled back loosely in a ribbon. The ends of the ribbon may be shown floating in the air behind them, suggesting their alert receptivity to God's command.

We read in Scripture about Michael, Gabriel, and other angels, including the seraphim in Isaiah 6. Jesus tells us that they rejoice over every sinner that repents, and that each person has a guardian angel who always beholds the face of the Father (Matt. 18:10). But beyond that, angels remain mysterious. We get the impression that a whole lot more is going on with them than we know about. Probably we know all we need to. There is a temptation to make angels objects of fascination, because we humans persistently desire to have contact with the supernatural without having to deal with God and all His bothersome ethical requirements. However, there is no such thing as a freelance angel, and people who think they're regularly talking to one are dealing with something other than an angel.

On this gray day in early November we have been walking around the church, noticing the many angels holding down official positions on the iconostasis and elsewhere. But here in the back, on the wall behind the choir's music stands, we find a collection of icons that includes a particularly striking angel, the first of our black-and-white plates. It's called the "Angel with the Golden Hair" and shows Gabriel in prayer. Like St. John the Baptist on the iconostasis, he comes originally from a deisis, a set of icons depicting figures turning toward Christ in supplication. This is a twelfth-century Russian icon, like the Virgin of Vladimir, and the two are similar in style. Gabriel's eyes are patient and receptive, and there is a rosy glow on his cheek and lips that matches his red tunic. Most distinctive, of course, are the fine threads of gold that run all through his auburn hair. He is crowned with a bright red jewel, the brightest point of the icon, which shines in a golden setting.

Gabriel is surrounded by a number of icons, and there doesn't seem to be a theme to this gathering. Apparently they're just ones that members of this congregation are fond of and have donated over the years. The only guiding principle of arrangement seems to be "the more the merrier."

Someone liked this icon of the Angel with the Golden Hair and placed it here on the back wall of the church. It's easy to see why: The angel is so completely absorbed in gazing at Christ that he isn't thinking about anything else. It's pleasant to look at someone who isn't looking back at us. As we fall into these wide, dark eyes we get caught up in his tranquil attention and lifted out of ourselves, which always feels like a relief.

It would be nice to have this kind of prayerful concentration always, the kind that comes so naturally to Gabriel. Most of the time, even at worship, our minds are jumbled with a thousand other things. Throughout the ancient liturgy are regular reminders to pay attention. "Let us stand upright! Let us stand with fear! Let us attend!" the deacon is instructed to say, and often he's saying it to himself as much as to anyone else. The main thing we know about the angels is, they're always paying attention. Even when scooping a child out of the path of an oncoming car, they are still rapt in worship, beholding the face of the Father.

At the midpoint of the ancient Eucharistic liturgy the congregation sings the Cherubic Hymn. The point of this hymn is to remind us to pay attention. We are getting ready to sing "Holy, Holy, Holy," as Isaiah heard the angels do around God's throne, and like them we must gather all our attention and put aside all earthly cares. So we sing the Cherubic Hymn slowly over and over, trying to work it down into our hearts.

In a Tolstoy short story a businessman admits to himself that his mind is always wandering to money matters, even during the singing of the Cherubic Hymn. Western readers may not catch that reference, but Tolstoy's original readers would know that this was the one point in the week, at least, when you were supposed to forget all the pestering worries of everyday life and, like Gabriel, give wholehearted attention to the Lord.

The Cherubic Hymn

Let us who mystically
represent
the cherubim
and who sing the thrice-holy hymn
to the life-creating Trinity
now lay aside all earthly cares

that we may receive the King of all
Who comes invisibly upborne
by the angelic hosts.

Alleluia! Alleluia! Alleluia!

CHAPTER SIX

The Annunciation

As we come in the church this evening we stop at the small stand set up right inside the entrance. Here is where the church displays the icon appropriate to the feast day currently being celebrated, which is why it's called a *festal* icon. When worshipers come in, they will venerate the icon, crossing themselves and kissing it. It's now March 25, exactly nine months before Christmas, so the festal icon on display shows the moment when Gabriel announced to the Virgin Mary that she would bear a child, an event called the Annunciation. This fourteenth-century icon (the second of our black-and-white plates) comes from a church in Ochrid, a city in Macedonia.

We had noticed in previous icons reverse perspective, which puts the vanishing point out where the viewer is standing. This icon does the opposite, with dramatically diminishing perspective collapsing toward the recoiling figure of the Virgin. The projecting canopy above her marble enclosure slants upwards, and the platform beneath her feet slants downwards, framing her in a rectangle that funnels our attention toward her precipitously. The plunge is halted by her uplifted hand, which hangs suspended at the center of the arrangement. In a moment she will say yes.

Gabriel is advancing toward her vigorously, which must have been an alarming sight. His muscular feet push off from the floor, and his wings are askew. He is bringing news of a great blessing, and bringing it urgently, with hair ribbons flying and fingertips outstretched. This is a busy, tumultuous scene.

Only secondarily do we notice the facial expressions on these two. Gabriel looks thoughtful and kind, and regards Mary with something like admiration. Mary, despite her posture, looks quietly pleased. Despite the whirl of the immediate moment, both are suspended in the tranquil joy at the timeless center of God's will.

In this icon it's hard to tell where, exactly, things are happening, and even hard to tell whether we're in or out of doors. The sky, or possibly the wall, is solid gold. Behind Gabriel a bit of architecture confuses the eye with multiple planes, like a castle by M. C. Escher. It is the red canopy that is the tip-off. There is never a ceiling in an icon; even events that indisputably occurred indoors were not concealed from the eternal gaze. From God's perspective, no room in the world has a ceiling. The convention in icons is to indicate that an event took place indoors by draping a length of cloth over the top of the scene.

March 25 usually comes in Lent, the seven-week season before Pascha. Most church members look forward to Lent, even though it entails a great deal more prayer and fasting. It feels like spiritual housecleaning. Fasting is not punishment, but a kind of physical prayer, like weightlifting, to strengthen the willpower muscle. Unless it is part of an entire program of corporate and private prayer, fasting is meaningless.

One of the additional prayer services of the season is the Akathist Hymn, which is sung on Friday nights. "Akathist" means "not sitting," so this hymn is sung with everyone standing. It was written by St. Romanos the Melodist, a Syrian monk of the sixth century.

According to the story, St. Romanos had served as a deacon in Beirut before moving to Constantinople, where he was derided by sophisticated clergy for his backward ways and musical ineptitude. One Christmas Eve Romanos fell asleep weeping over this bullying, then saw in a dream the Virgin handing him a scroll and telling him to swallow it. In the morning he went into church for the Christmas service, walked forward to stand in front of the iconostasis, and sang a hymn that has been used ever after as the *kontakion*, or main hymn, of the day. We'll hear this hymn in the next chapter, when we look at the icon of the Nativity. Romanos went on to write hundreds of exquisitely beautiful hymns, including this Akathist chanted on Friday nights in Lent. It begins with a section recounting the Annunciation, which brings to life the scene in our icon this evening.

An angel chieftain was sent from heaven to say "Hail!" to the Theotokos. And beholding You, O Lord, taking bodily form, he stood rapt in wonder, and with bodiless voice cried aloud to her:

Hail, you through whom joy shall shine forth; Hail, you through whom the curse shall be destroyed.

Hail, restoration of fallen Adam; Hail, redemption of the tears of Eve.

Hail, height untrod by human minds; Hail, depth hard to scan, even for angels' eyes.

Hail, you who are a kingly throne; Hail, you who hold the Upholder of all.

Hail, star that showed the Sun; Hail, Womb of the divine incarnation.

Hail, you through whom Creation is renewed; Hail, you through whom the Creator becomes a babe.

Hail, O Bride without bridegroom!

Boldly spake the holy maiden spoke unto Gabriel, conscious of her chastity: To my soul your strange message seems hard to grasp; how do you speak of a virgin conception, Alleluia.

Craving to know knowledge unknowable, the Virgin cried out unto him who ministered to her: From a maiden body, how may a Son be born, tell me! To her he spoke in fear, and thus only cried aloud:

Hail, initiate of the ineffable counsel; Hail, faith of those who pray in silence.

Hail, beginning of the miracles of Christ; Hail, crown of his decrees.

Hail, heavenly ladder, by which God came down; Hail, Bridge that leads us from earth to heaven.

Hail, much-talked-of wonder of angels; Hail, much-lamented damager of demons.

Hail, you who ineffably bore the Light; Hail, you who told none how it was done.

Hail, you who oversoar the knowledge of the wise; Hail, you who enlighten the minds of the faithful.

Hail, O Bride without bridegroom!

Divine power from on high then overshadowed the maiden, that she might conceive, and showed forth her fruitful womb as a fertile field to all who desire to reap salvation, as they sing: Alleluia.

CHAPTER SEVEN

The Nativity

You would know that it's Christmas, even if you missed noticing the icon on the stand: The church is overflowing with poinsettias and red and gold ribbons, and an evergreen garland has been woven all along the top of the iconostasis. The congregation begins to gather at 9:00 P.M., expecting to receive Communion a little after midnight. The smallest children are arriving in footed blanket-sleepers, as at the Pascha service. Christmas comes at the end of another fast, one that began in mid-November, so worshipers are looking forward to a first taste of eggnog and butter cookies after the service.

The icon on the stand (the third of our black-and-white plates) is another from St. Catherine's monastery on Mt. Sinai, but it looks very different from the Christ of Sinai on the iconostasis, even though it was made about the same time. The rendering of the images is simpler, less detailed, and the faces are rounded and somewhat childlike. Perhaps it was made locally in Sinai, rather than by professional iconographers from Constantinople. Icons from North Africa, from Ethiopia or Egypt, often have this distinctive rounded look; a Russian face, like that of the Virgin of Vladimir, will be longer.

The other notable thing about this icon is that a great deal is going on at once. In the center, Mary lies in a cave with her swaddled Son beside her. Icons show the Nativity occurring in a cave rather than a wood-frame stable; in ancient Israel trees were scarce and wooden construction rare, not to be wasted on animals. The blackness of the cave recalls the black pit under Christ's feet in the icon of the Resurrection, but here it is dotted with stars. Mary lies down, rather than kneeling by the manger, and gazes out solemnly as if pondering these things in her heart. There is a donkey at the end of the manger with his tongue stuck out, perhaps nudging the baby aside in search of hay, and a cow with crescent horns faces us, apparently smiling.

Joseph did not attend the birth; instead, two midwives assisted, and they are seen in the lower right bathing the baby Jesus. In a narrative icon it is not unusual for the same character to appear more than once. Joseph is a white-haired old man; early Christian writings describe him as an elderly relative of Mary's, a widower with grown children. In the icon he is sitting in another cave on the lower left, waiting to be told he can come back, and he looks distinctly miserable. In some stories, Satan came to him during this interval in the guise of an old shepherd, and asked insinuatingly, "You don't really believe all this stuff about a virgin birth, do you?" Joseph represents all those who, at the doorstep of miracle, are tempted to fall back into doubt. In some icons of the Nativity we see Mary's gaze directed toward him in patient compassion, modeling how we should treat those who question our faith, or who struggle to believe.

114

Shepherds and black-and-white sheep are threaded through the scene, and one sheep runs over the feet of the first of the three Wise Men, who are arriving on the right, bearing gifts. The Wise Men's three horses appear below left, next to Joseph. Overhead the golden skies are full of angels, three lifting their hands to heaven and one leaning down to tell those of us on earth.

No wonder the icon is busy; the story is busy. On the scroll that the Virgin Mary gave Romanos in his dream was written this hymn:

> The Virgin brings forth today
> the Word Eternal
> and the earth offers a cave
> to the Unapproachable.
> Angels give glory with shepherds,
> and the Magi journey with the star,
> when for our sakes was born
> as a new babe
> He who is from eternity God.

Themes keep recurring throughout the ancient Nativity hymns: that the God whom all the universe could not hold was contained in a small cave; that glorious angels sing in chorus with rustic shepherds; that the Wise Men, astrologers "who worshiped the stars, learned from them to worship [Christ], the Sun of Justice."

And in all this Joseph sits, troubled. He hasn't seen the baby yet, or the angels, or the Wise Men. He doesn't know that soon the baby's life will be threatened by Herod, and that he will have to lead his family into Egypt to save them. A lot of difficult and barely comprehensible things are about to happen to this old man, Joseph.

Like Mary in the Annunciation, this is his moment of submission to God's will. After this point in the Gospel we hear less and less about Joseph. But when he gets up and goes back to the cave, he will be agreeing to do whatever God requires of him, in this whole startling conclusion to his hitherto quiet life. This is why they call it a leap of faith; you don't always know what you're getting into. That's why doubt is a good thing, in some respects. You should look before you leap; as

Jesus said, you should be sure that you are ready to put your hand to the plow and not look back. He calls this "counting the cost." It's not out of place to include in an icon a man who is wrestling with doubts.

This morning, the morning of Christmas Eve, a smaller portion of the congregation assembled for the service called the "Royal Hours." Monasteries observe eight times of prayer each day, termed the "Hours"; the service of the Royal Hours goes through the first four Hours of Christmas Eve back-to-back, an arrangement originally provided for the convenience of visiting royalty who then would not have to wait around for the next service to begin. As we approach this event full to overflowing with astonished, busy joy, the service lets lingering doubt speak in counterpoint as well.

From the Royal Hours of the Eve of the Nativity

Make ready, O Bethlehem:
let the manger be prepared,
let the cave show its welcome!

117

The truth comes and the shadow flees!
God is born of a virgin, and is revealed to men.
He is clothed in our flesh, and makes it divine.
Therefore Adam is renewed,
and cries out with Eve,
"Your favor has appeared on earth, O Lord,
For the salvation of the human race!"

Joseph said to the Virgin,
"What has happened to you, O Mary?
I am troubled;
what can I say to you?
Doubt clouds my mind. Depart from me!
What has happened to you, O Mary?
Instead of honor, you bring me shame.
Instead of joy, you fill me with grief.
Men who praised me will blame me.
I cannot bear condemnation on every side.
I received you, a pure virgin in the sight of
the Lord.
What is this now I see?"

Before Your birth, O Lord,
the hosts of angels already perceived the
mystery.

They were struck with wonder and trembled,
for You Who adorned the heavens with stars
are now well-pleased to be born as a babe.
You hold the ends of the earth in Your hands,
but now You are laid in a manger of dumb
 beasts.
Yet all these things fulfilled Your saving plan,
by which Your compassion was revealed to us.
O Christ of great mercy, glory to You!

Mary was of David's seed, so she went with
Joseph to register in Bethlehem.
She bore in her womb the fruit
 not sown by man.
The time for the birth was at hand.
Since there was no room at the inn, the cave
became a beautiful palace for the queen.
Christ is born, raising the image that fell of
old!

When Joseph went up to Bethlehem,
His heart was filled with sadness.
But you cried out to him, O Virgin,
"Why are you so troubled?
Why are you in misery, seeing me with child?

Do you not understand at all?
I bear a fearful mystery!
Cast your fears away,
  and learn a strange wonder:
God in His mercy
  descends from heaven to earth.
Within my womb He has taken flesh!
When He is pleased to be born,
  you will see Him.
You will rejoice, and worship your Creator.
The angels ceaselessly praise Him in song,
glorifying Him with the Father and the
  Holy Spirit."

CHAPTER EIGHT

The Theophany

The church year allows a full nine months, from the Annunciation on March 25 to the Nativity on December 25, for the Virgin's pregnancy and birth. But less than two weeks after we celebrate Jesus' birth we are at a feast commemorating an event that took place many years later. Today we are standing with the Lord on the banks of the Jordan, where an incredulous John the Baptist is hearing Jesus' request to be baptized.

As worshipers come in for the service on the eve of the January 6 feast, they see on the icon stand an image of Jesus standing in a tide of rushing dark water, while His cousin John stretches on tiptoe to gingerly reach His head. This feast is significant because it is the first revelation of the Trinity, as the Father speaks and the Spirit visibly descends on the

Son. The day is called either *Epiphany* or *Theophany*, words indicating the showing-forth or manifestation of God.

The Baptism is also seen as a charge to use water in blessing, so during the Theophany service a large quantity of water is set aside and prayed over. The chalice-shaped font is moved to the center of the church and filled to the brim; during the service lessons from Isaiah are read, and the priest prays over the font and dips a cross into the water. The water will be used throughout the year at services that call for sprinkling of holy water, and worshipers will also take home bottles for private use; some sip a little each day during their prayers. Every home will be blessed during the next month. The family leads the priest all through their home, holding candles and the icon of this feast, while he sprinkles the walls with holy water. All sing the Troparion of Theophany:

When You, O Lord, were baptized in the Jordan, the worship of the Trinity was made manifest.

For the voice of the Father bore witness to
You and called You His beloved Son.
And the Spirit in the form of a dove
  confirmed the truthfulness of His word.
O Christ our God, who has revealed Yourself
and has enlightened the world, glory to You!

This icon (the fourth of our black-and-white
plates) is Greek, from the early seventeenth
century, and it shows a symmetrically divided
scene with John on the left and four angels on
the right. Three are looking on the scene,
while one turns to look upward toward the
Father's voice. In some icons, the Father's
presence will be shown as a half-circle at the
top of the icon, indicating that the divine
presence continues far beyond our compre-
hension. A line of light extends downward,
and in it we see the dove. There is a principle
in iconography that images are to be confined
to what God has actually deigned to show us;
we are not to make speculative pictures, such
as the print I've seen in gift shops showing
Jesus in heaven happily hugging a new arrival.
While popular imagination pictures the

123

Father as an old man with a beard, He has never revealed Himself in that form, and images depicting Him that way fall outside the icon tradition.

The whole scene is enclosed by towering rocks, as in the icon of the Resurrection. The water is glossy and dark, and at the bottom we see a figure of an old man pouring the river out of a terracotta jug. He is there to represent the words of Psalm 114:3, "The sea looked and fled, Jordan turned back."

The feast of Theophany has been observed since the early days of the church, and during the service of the Blessing of the Waters the priest will read a prayer written by St. Sophronius, the patriarch of Jerusalem in the seventh century. This prayer captures an additional meaning of Theophany: that not only is Jesus revealed as God incarnate, but that all creation is shown to be His, and to be capable of bearing His grace-filled presence. In a way, this feast is a further endorsement of the goodness of matter that we see affirmed in iconography itself and in the Incarnation. We can make icons out of wood and paint, we can pray over water and use it in blessing, we can even bless the walls of our homes, because material creation is very good and nothing in it is outside God's rule. He created it, He claimed it, and He became human to dwell in it. We don't have a religion that teaches a separation between Holy Stuff and the rest of life; everything belongs to Him and is filled with His presence—even something as basic, simple, and ordinary as water.

From the Theophany prayer of St. Sophronius

Today the grace of the Holy Spirit has
    descended on the waters in the likeness
    of a dove.
Today has shone the sun that does not set,
    and the world is lighted by the light of the
    Lord.
Today the moon shines with the world in its
    radiating beams.
Today the shining stars adorn the universe
    with the splendor of their radiance.
Today the clouds from heaven moisten
    mankind with showers of justice.

Today the Uncreated accepts of His own will
  the laying on of hands by His own creation.
Today the Prophet and Forerunner draws
  nigh to the Master, and halts with trembling
  when he witnesses the condescension of God
  towards us.
Today the waters of the Jordan are changed
  to healing by the presence of the Lord.
Today the whole universe is watered
  by mystical streams.
Today the sins of mankind are blotted out by
  the waters of the Jordan.
Today the darkness of the world vanishes
  with the appearance of our God.
Today the whole creation is lighted from on
  high.
Today is error annulled, and the coming of
  the Lord prepares for us a way of salvation.
Today the celestials celebrate with the
  terrestrials, and the terrestrials commune
  with the celestials.
Today the assembly of noble and great-voiced
  Orthodoxy rejoices.
Today the Lord comes to baptism to elevate
  mankind above.

Today the Unbowable bows to His servant
to deliver us from slavery.
Today we have bought the kingdom of heaven,
for the kingdom of heaven has no end.

Jordan turned back and the mountains shouted
with joy at beholding God in the flesh. And
the clouds gave voice, wondering at Him who
comes, who is Light of Light, true God of true
God, drowning in the Jordan the death of sin,
the thorn of error, and bond of Hades,
granting the world the baptism of salvation.

So also I, Your unworthy sinning servant, as I
proclaim Your great wonders, am encompassed
by fear, crying reverently unto You, and
saying:

Great are You, O Lord, and marvelous are
Your works, and there is no word which is
sufficient to hymn Your wonders!

Great are You, O Lord, and marvelous are
Your works, and there is no word which is
sufficient to hymn Your wonders!

Great are You, O Lord, and marvelous are Your works, and there is no word which is sufficient to hymn Your wonders!

CHAPTER NINE

The Transfiguration

Once again we are visiting Holy Resurrection on an evening in early August, this time for the feast of the Transfiguration. Scripture tells us that Jesus went up on Mt. Tabor with three of His disciples, Peter, James, and John. "And He was transfigured before them, and His face shone like the sun, and His garments became white as light" (Matt. 17:2). The great prophets Moses and Elijah appeared beside Him, speaking to Him. Peter offered to build shelters for the three of them, "not knowing what he said" and babbling the first excited thing that came to mind. Then the Father's voice was heard from heaven, echoing His words at the Baptism: "This is my beloved Son, with whom I am well-pleased; listen to Him" (Matt. 17:5). At that the disciples fell down in fear and awe. When

Jesus came and raised them up again, they discovered everything as it was before.

This icon (the fifth of our black-and-white plates) is another early one from St. Catherine's monastery on Mt. Sinai, like the icon of Christ on the iconostasis, and the icon of the Nativity we looked at in the seventh chapter. This icon also dates from the mid-sixth century and was made when the monastery church was originally built. However, it differs from the other two icons in one notable respect: It is executed in mosaic, not painted. Tiny colored pieces of glass, called *tesserae*, are set in place to create the image. It is, of course, much more difficult to make an icon this way, and the flowing movement a paintbrush readily achieves can be elusive unless the tesserae are tiny.

Yet mosaics have the advantage of being nearly impervious to time. As long as they stick to the wall, their color will not dim, and smoke and grime can be cleaned off the glass surface without damaging the underlying image. The glass gives off a shimmering light, especially when the tesserae are carefully set to reflect at subtly different angles. Mosaic icons give us our best opportunity to see how icons were intended to look when new.

This mosaic fills the apse over the altar of the monastery church, so it is applied to a curved ceiling and not flat as it appears here. The row of round icons over Christ's head curve in a vertical half-circle, running along the underside of the arch above the altar; the row beneath His feet curve in a horizontal half-circle, running along the back wall as the lower border of the icon. Christ himself fills the center of the curve of the apse, standing in a deep blue, full-body mandorla. Elijah is on His right and Moses on His left, while James and John fall back in awe, and Peter lies prostrate at the bottom of the scene.

One of the extraordinary achievements of this icon is that it appears, when viewed straight-on like this, to be flat. It is difficult to design an icon for a dome or apse, because the concave surface can throw elements out of proportion, causing them to bulge or to shrink. For example, if you are looking at an icon of Christ in a steep dome, the elements at the outer edge, like His hand, would appear huge, while elements in the middle, like His face, would appear tiny, unless the iconographer has planned ahead for the problem. No matter what shape the underlying surface, the finished image needs to appear in proportion; in effect, it should appear flat, like a portrait or window. The iconographers who produced this ancient mosaic icon compensated for the curve so skillfully that when viewed directly, as in this photograph, the bowl of the apse is imperceptible.

Worshipers come to this evening service bearing baskets of fruit, especially grapes. In ancient times this feast was associated with the first harvests of summer, and at the end of the service the fruit is blessed. There are also prayers that the herbs presented would be effective for healing those who use them; these prayers come from a time when most medicine came from plants. Transfigurations are everywhere: grapes become wine, and wine becomes the Eucharistic blood; herbs become medicine, which becomes renewed strength in those who use them. Everywhere,

God is working through His creation. As with the water blessed at Theophany, no element of material creation is too humble to bear His imprint.

Peter, James, and John, tumbled on the ground before their transfigured Lord, are also going to be made into something else. The Transfiguration is our destiny as well. When we drink the wine made Eucharistic blood it changes us, and we become "partakers of the divine nature" (2 Pet. 1:4), alight with the presence of Christ. This light of Mt. Tabor will shine through us, as in the Burning Bush, illuminating without consuming. At this moment on the mountain, Christ revealed to the disciples a glimpse, only as much as they could stand to see, of what we're all journeying toward.

The Transfiguration is said to have occurred forty days before the Crucifixion, so that when that terrifying day came they would know, at least, that Jesus went to the Cross under His own power and of His own free will. Anyone who can manifest this kind of transformation has no need to go along quietly when people come out against Him with swords and clubs (Luke 22:52), not unless He wants to go. The disciples would know that the Cross must not be the end of the story. There must be that something that lay in store beyond it—not just for Jesus, but for all of us.

The Kontakion of the Transfiguration

You were transfigured on the mount,
and Your disciples beheld Your glory
as far as they could bear it,
O Christ our God;
so that, when they should see You crucified,
they would remember that
Your suffering was voluntary,
and could declare to all the world
that You are truly the radiant splendor
of the Father.

CHAPTER TEN

The Crucifixion

As the congregation comes in this Thursday evening in spring we notice that some of them look very tired. Lent has been going on a long time now, with many additional services of deeply moving intensity. The season began more than six weeks ago with Forgiveness Vespers, the annual service in which each person in the congregation asks forgiveness from every other person. Making a deep bow, or even dropping to the floor in a prostration, each says in his own words, "Forgive me." Some expand and personalize this request: "Please forgive me, my sister, for any way I have sinned against you," or "My brother in Christ, please forgive all the ways I have offended you." One woman says, "Forgive all the ways my sins pollute the world you have to live in." There are many tears and much embracing. Mothers ask their children for forgiveness, and toddlers say to teenagers, "Forgive?" Thus cleansed and reconciled, the community is ready to begin their community pilgrimage through the desert days of Lent.

The last week before Pascha, Holy Week, introduces a heightened intensity. Now there are one or more services every day, some of which last several hours, all of which include ancient hymns of piercing beauty. People look forward to this week all year, although they know it will take a lot out of them. But the experience is so spiritually revitalizing that some take the week off from work, in order to savor every minute.

The people coming in on this Thursday night have seen a lot of each other recently. There have been services every night since the previous Friday, and some mornings as well, with everything building toward the Pascha liturgy that will begin at midnight Saturday. You get to know people very well when you spend this much time with them, especially if you are tired and hungry, and that covering of forgiveness almost seven weeks ago is becoming increasingly indispensable. This evening's service is known as "The Passion Gospels," and over the course of three hours the entire Passion story will be read, covering the Passion narratives from all four Gospels in a series of twelve readings.

It is with the fifth reading that we reach the moment when "they led Him away to be crucified." Those few, stark words conjure a primal image in the mind of every Christian. Yet where does that image come from? Scripture's details are scant. We have made a composite picture from the many depictions we have seen in painting, sculpture, and film. While those images display some variety of interpretation, icons of the Crucifixion follow a single pattern.

An iconographer does not seek to express personal creative vision, but to vanish behind the spiritual beauty of what is depicted. After consulting previous versions of the scene, the iconographer approaches the task with prayer and fasting. Most icons are unsigned. Variation is not shown by original arrangements of elements, but through subtly differing use of light, color, perspective, and expression.

The icon we see tonight (the sixth of our black-and-white plates) shows a startling contrast of black against gold, as the Cross rises up dramatically to divide the scene. Christ is enthroned on the Cross; He suffers for our sakes, but He has chosen to suffer, and brings to this moment a regal dignity. This is the same Christ whom we saw transfigured in glory, and who could call on ten thousand legions of angels if He chose. No power on earth holds Him to the Cross but His own will.

This icon was painted by Emmanuel Lambardos, a native of Crete. We know exactly when, because he inscribed the names of the donors next to their tiny kneeling figures at the bottom of the icon. These are a father and son, a lawyer and a poet, and the icon was painted between 1613 and 1618.

Lambardos has arranged the major figures according to traditional pattern, with Mary on the left looking up toward Jesus, and John the Beloved Disciple on the right, looking down in sorrow. The women who will bring spices to the empty tomb, called the Myrrh-Bearing Women, surround Mary. Mary Magdalene, in an orange robe and with her long hair characteristically loose, is leaning over the grieving mother and giving her a consoling embrace. Behind John, Longinus the Centurion looks up in amazement: "Surely, this was the Son of God!"

Beneath the foot of the Cross we see into a black pit, in which there is a skull. Golgotha (or Calvary) means "the place of a skull," and it is likely that bones could be seen in this place outside the city walls, where criminals were executed and where there were tombs. In the icon, the skull at the base of the Cross is Adam's. Jesus' blood runs down to anoint the skull, delivering us all from imprisonment in Hades.

This icon shows the other side of the events in the icon of the Resurrection, on the far left of the iconostasis (and the first of the color panels). There we could see that Jesus' sacrificial death on the Cross had brought Him into Hades, where He could free us from the bondage of sin. He begins with Adam, seizing Him by the wrist and hauling Him out of his tomb, the same Adam whose skull lays here at the foot of the Cross. The wood of the Cross recalls the wood of the Tree of Life; when Adam ate of that fruit we were all made captive to sin, but when Jesus ascended the Tree of the Cross, He set us free. The parallels between the "Old Adam" and the "New Adam," explored so eloquently by St. Paul, were continued in vital form in the prayers and iconography of the early Christians.

You'll notice that the use of blood here is restrained, almost delicate; the parallel stripes of golden red that flow from Jesus' feet are laid down like threads. Icons do not show Jesus writhing in agony or excessively gory, as was sometimes done in Western art. In general, icons do not aim at deliberate emotional effect, which can slide so easily into sentimentality. While there is no doubt that Christ's Passion involved real, and even gruesome, suffering, Jesus undertook it with divine dignity and of His own will. So this doesn't look as "emotional" as you might expect a picture of the Crucifixion to look. The emotional power of a Crucifixion icon depends less on our empathizing with how such physical pain would have felt to us, and more on our awe-filled recognition of something we cannot understand at all by mere empathy: How could God, the God of all Creation and our Creator, undertake such suffering for us? In an icon Christ's humanity and divinity are kept in balance, and we wonder at this juxtaposition of His kingly power and voluntary debasement. The angels, who comprehend His glory far better than we do, react with amazement and awe.

In the church an empty wooden cross, about six feet tall, is standing in front of the iconostasis. After the fifth Gospel reading the lights are turned low and the people kneel. The priest lifts the cross, then begins a slow procession through the church, preceded by altar boys with candles and incense.

When the priest returns to the front of the church he lays the cross upon the floor, then places on top of it an icon cut out in the form of the crucified body of Christ. He lays this corpus upon the wooden cross and, with ringing blows, drives a nail through each hand and foot. The room is hushed and still, but you can hear that some are struggling with tears. In the silence a single chanter lifts up his clear tenor voice in this hymn:

The Fifteenth Antiphon of Great and Holy Thursday

Today He who hung the earth upon the waters
   is hung upon a tree.

The King of the Angels
   is crowned with thorns.

He who covered the heavens with clouds
   is robed in the purple of mockery.

He who delivered Adam in the Jordan
   is slapped on the face.

The Bridegroom of the Church
   is fastened with nails.

The Son of the Virgin
  is pierced with a spear.

We adore Your sufferings, O Christ.

Show us also Your glorious Resurrection.

She who gave birth to You cries aloud saying,
  "What strange mystery do I behold,
  O my Son?
How have You died, elevated on the Tree,
  O You who give and grant life?"

CHAPTER ELEVEN

The Epitaphios

Just one day later we have gathered in church again, this time for a Friday evening service commemorating Jesus' burial. The icon of this moment is called the "Epitaphios," and our version, like the Crucifixion icon in the chapter before, was painted by Emmanuel Lambardos. This icon (the seventh of our black-and-white plates) is crowded with people bending low over the form of Jesus, who is laid out at the foot of the Cross on a red marble slab. His mother leans over Him, cradling His head. John the Beloved Disciple also bends forward, and at Jesus' feet Joseph of Arimathea, who gave his tomb, lifts the shroud to wrap Him. Nicodemus, the ruler of the synagogue who came to Jesus by night, leans on the ladder he had used to reach and pull the nails from the Cross. A huddled circle

144

of Myrrh-Bearing Women kneel behind the Virgin; Mary Magdalene, robed in brilliant red, has thrown her arms into the air. Above them all the low, black arms of the Cross emphasize the horizontal line of their bowed heads and bodies.

We gather this evening for a service called the "Lamentations," that will have at its center a procession involving an icon of the Epitaphios. This will not be the one on the icon stand, but a larger similar one executed in needlepoint, a rectangle measuring about three feet by four feet, trimmed with a heavy golden fringe. The central scene resembles the Lambardos icon in its arrangement of the figures, and around them appears this hymn honoring Joseph of Arimathea: "Noble Joseph, having taken Thy pure body down from the tree, wrapped it in linen with spices, and laid it in a new tomb."

When worshipers enter the church this evening all signs of the Crucifixion are gone. Instead there is a wooden bier with two tiers, the top standing about four feet high and covered with flowers. On the lower platform

145

is laid the needlepointed Epitaphios icon, as if it is Jesus' body prepared for burial. At one point in the service, four men of the church then lift the bier to their shoulders and carry it outside, into the night. The congregation follows, holding candles and singing in a minor key, "Holy God, Holy Mighty, Holy Immortal, have mercy on us." As with the previous night's Crucifixion, tonight they are acting out the events depicted in the Epitaphios icon. The whole congregation follows the bier around the exterior of the church, as if it were a funeral procession.

When the men return to the church door they stop and lift up the bier; worshipers bow to pass under it, returning to the nave of the church. The men then carry the bier back inside and place it before the iconostasis.

The event this icon depicts must have been the most desolate moment in Christian history. Jesus' followers had seen Him do great things and expected that still more glorious moments lay ahead. He himself had told them so. No doubt they had learned that His words were sometimes cryptic and not always to be taken at face value. Perhaps they thought this when He spoke of His own death, and presumed He was speaking symbolically. It made no sense for Him to be dead, as He so indisputably is here, cold and stiff. How could that be part of the plan? Whatever was to happen next depended on Jesus; they had no other hope. Yet He was as unresponsive as a corpse.

In this one terrible moment doubt must have swept in like a black cloud. Imagine that the story stops here, with St. Mary Magdalene wailing in grief. If we froze time at this moment and imagine that Jesus did not rise from the dead, how would the world have been different? How would your life be different?

"If Christ has not been raised, then our preaching is in vain and your faith is in vain," Paul wrote (1 Cor. 15:14). Imagine that: The whole of Christian history, every act of kindness or justice, every sermon preached, every orphanage built, every slave freed, everything ever done in the name of Christ would be a sham. The great music inspired by

147

the love of Christ would be a fruit of delusion. The martyrs' deaths would be a kind of horrible joke. "We are even found to be misrepresenting God, because we testified of God that He raised Christ," Paul continues (1 Cor. 15:15). Not only is our work futile, but we're even telling lies about God. "If for this life only we have hoped in Christ, we are of all men most to be pitied" (1 Cor. 15:19). Others should treat us with condescending sympathy, because we have wholly abandoned ourselves to a hope that is absurd.

If that was the end of the story, the scene in this icon would be unbearably bitter, ludicrous, and meaningless. "But in fact Christ has been raised from the dead, the first fruits of those who have fallen asleep," Paul concludes (1 Cor. 15:20). This is not the end of the story, and it is only because we know the ending that we can allow ourselves to endure this piercing grief tonight.

Before this procession the congregation gathered around the bier, holding lit candles, and sang the ancient Lamentations. It is one stop in a very crowded week. After this service, some will stay all night in church keeping vigil by the bier, while others set their alarms to drive over for a visit at two or three in the morning. The community will gather tomorrow morning for another Eucharist, and once more for the Paschal liturgy tomorrow night.

It has been a long week and they are tired. But for just a moment at the end of this service each person will kneel before the bier and lean in to kiss the icon. It is like leaning into a dark, flower-filled cave. Jesus, who appears in this icon so wasted and spent, will arise again to glorious life, and raise us all with Him. But tonight we stop for a moment and wait beside the bier. The words of the Lamentations express the grief of those gathered around His body, in this icon and in this congregation.

From the Lamentations

In a grave they laid You, O my Life and my Christ, and the armies of the angels were so amazed as they sang the praise of Your submissive love.

149

O my sweet Lord Jesus, my salvation and my light, how are You now by a grave and all its darkness hid? How unspeakable the mystery of Your love!

"Gone the light the world knew, gone the light that was mine, O my Jesus who are all of my heart's desire," so the Virgin spoke lamenting at Your grave.

"Who will give me water for the tears I must weep?" So the maiden wed to God cried with loud lament, "that for my sweet Jesus I may rightly mourn."

"Ah, Your eyes so sweet, and Your lips, O Word, how shall I close them? How the dues of death shall I pay to You?" So cried Joseph as he shook with holy fear.

Dirges at the tomb goodly Joseph sings with Nicodemus, bringing praise to Christ who by men was slain, and in song with them are joined the seraphim.

150

Every generation
to Your grave comes bringing,
dear Christ, its dirge of praises.

Women bringing spices
came with loving forethought
Your due of myrrh to give You.

Joseph is entombing,
helped by Nicodemus,
the body of his Maker.

Myrrh the women sprinkled,
store of spices bringing
to grace Your tomb ere dawning.

Hasten, Word, Your rising,
and release from sorrow
the spotless maid that bore You.

O Triune Godhead,
Father, Son, and Spirit,
upon the world have mercy.

CHAPTER TWELVE

The Old Testament Trinity

Lent and Holy Week culminate in Pascha, which is too big to last just one day, but goes on for many weeks. The first week of Pascha is called "Bright Week," in recognition of its inaugural place in the course of "this pure and radiant feast." For the entire season of Pascha no kneeling is allowed, and penitential hymns and prayers are dismissed. Then, on the evening of Pentecost, a service of Vespers with "the Kneeling Prayers" reintroduces the balance of repentance and gratitude, sorrow and joy.

Pentecost is the feast of the Descent of the Holy Spirit, and since the Spirit is associated with life and growing things, the church is decked with greenery. Potted plants have been arranged in front of the iconostasis, and vines looped over the tops of the windows.

Even the worshipers are wearing green shirts or dresses that they might not pull out of the closet any other time than St. Patrick's Day. The icon titled "The Descent of the Holy Spirit" shows the holy apostles seated in a semicircle, while rays of red light stream down toward them from a semicircle at the upper edge of the icon. Red scarves laid over the tops of the walls behind them let you know this event is happening indoors.

While that icon is a historical depiction of Pentecost, a different icon (the last of our black-and-white plates) is also used on the day of the feast of Pentecost. It is called the "Old Testament Trinity" and was painted by a gifted Russian monk named St. Andrei Rublev in 1411. The abbot of his monastery was the beloved spiritual father St. Sergius of Radonezh. When St. Sergius died, St. Andrei Rublev painted this icon to hang over Sergius's tomb in the cathedral at the monastery. Though he executed many beautiful icons, this one is acclaimed as his masterpiece and may be the best-known icon in the West.

What does the name "Old Testament Trinity" mean? Recall that we are not allowed to make icons of speculative scenes, but may reproduce only what God has seen fit to reveal in history. Scripture doesn't give us much to draw on, if we're looking for moments when all three persons of the Trinity were manifested simultaneously and visibly or audibly; Jesus' baptism in the Jordan is a rare exception.

The Old Testament Trinity is drawn from the visit of three angels to Abraham and Sarah in the eighteenth chapter of Genesis. Abraham was sitting at the door of his tent near the oaks of Mamre when he suddenly saw three men standing in front of him. He begged them to stay for a meal and stood by the tree while they ate the cakes Sarah hastily prepared, along with milk, curds, and roast calf. They told Abraham that Sarah would have a son in the spring, which made her laugh out loud since she and her husband were both very old. (She did have a son, and named him Isaac, meaning "laughter.") Then they told Abraham that they were next going to investigate the outcry against the city of Sodom.

When you read this passage in Genesis you notice that it switches from singular to plural in describing the visitors, from "men" to "LORD" (representing the never-spoken Hebrew name of God) to "angels." Three men come, but "the LORD appeared" to Abraham. "They" ask Abraham where his wife is, then "the LORD" announces that she will bear a son. At the end of the story, the men depart, while Abraham continues to stand "before the LORD." That evening, in Sodom, Lot rises to greet the travelers—but now they are neither three men nor "the LORD," but "two angels."

Whatever is going on here is complicated, and Scripture doesn't give us enough information to be sure we have it all straightened out. This much we rely on: The three men, or angels, who appeared to Abraham are a visitation by the Lord; God appeared in the form of three persons. Thus this icon shows them as angels seated around a table, of a kind that would have been familiar to Christians as an altar. The central angel gestures toward a chalice, which contains a dark red substance, perhaps wine or the calf sacrificed for their meal. A niche in the front of the altar is a miniature tomb where the relics of saints would be kept, a custom that began when the early Eucharists were celebrated at the burial place of martyrs in the catacombs. Behind the central angel we see the oak tree, which must have been a well-known landmark in that generally treeless land. In some versions of this icon we see Abraham and Sarah standing in the background, offering food on covered dishes; in such cases it is not called the "Old Testament Trinity" but "The Hospitality of Abraham."

Who are these three figures? Some would say that it overreaches to assign each one an identity; we should halt at the level of mystery and simply accept that the three together represent the Trinity. Others would note that the two on the right are clearly deferring to the figure on the left. He would be the Father, who is raising His hand to bless them. His robe is shimmering iridescent, golden-orange shifting to mossy green. The Son, in the middle, gestures toward the chalice of sacrifice and wears a robe of vibrant blue. The Spirit, on the right, is clothed in fresh green with yellow highlights. All three carry identical staffs, indicating their mutual authority. This icon is beloved because of its harmonious form and color, and because it conveys lightness and energy without a hint of sentiment.

The whole is so airy and translucent that we do seem to be looking through a window into heaven. On this side of the icon we still bear the marks of the earth from which we're made, and are not nearly so light. The green we wear for Pentecost looks decidedly earth-bound next to the Spirit's radiant robe. Three angels sit, almost float, around a heavenly altar, and our presence at this altar is not nearly so iridescent.

While the majestic, ethereal Old Testament Trinity is one icon used on the feast of Pentecost, the icon depicting the historical event shows a circle of rustic fishermen gathered in an upper room. They can hardly comprehend what has happened, and will happen, to them. Then they feel a rushing wind begin to blow.

It's a long way to go, to journey from one icon to another. It's a long way from the upper room to the heavenly altar where men, angels, and God gather. The humble fishermen will be set afire with the Spirit and will scatter to bring the gospel to often inhospitable lands. Most of them will die in miserable ways a long way from home. But that is how they reached their home, their true home. That is how they arrived on the other side of the window, where we all hope to be one day.

Troparion of Pentecost

Blessed art You, O Christ our God,
Who revealed the fishermen as all-wise
by sending down upon them the Holy Spirit,
and through them did draw the world
 into Your net.
O lover of mankind, glory to You!

On this June day we conclude a dozen visits to this small church, a dozen opportunities to gaze at "windows into heaven." These icons aren't just works of art, but ongoing stories that include us as well. We stand next to St. John the Baptist, learning how to pray with his intensity; we look at the wise eyes of our dear motherly friend the Virgin Mary and ask her to pray for us; we invite Jesus' profound gaze to search us and know us and make us whole. One way or another we can find ourselves in nearly every icon. There we are, like St. Mary Magdalene, turning away from the Crucifixion with tears streaming down our faces. Like James we kneel before the Transfiguration, thunderstruck. Like Adam, we feel Jesus pulling us up out of our tombs by a weak and helpless arm. Perhaps, like Joseph, we are sitting in a cave, wrestling with doubts.

As you continue to approach icons, come with an open heart, seeking to understand, and aware that you already "have been fully understood" (1 Cor. 13:12). Because a window has this distinctive feature: you can look through it from both sides.

GLOSSARY

Anastasis The Resurrection of Christ. In some contexts, may refer instead to the resurrection of the dead at the end of time.

Angel Doors Doors on the left and right ends of an iconostasis, which bear icons of angels. Alternatively, they may bear icons of sainted deacons, such as St. Stephen and St. Vincent, and be called "Deacons' Doors."

apse A semicircular projection in a wall, topped with a half-dome. In a church, the altar is often set under an apse in the east wall of the building.

deisis An iconic arrangement which shows Christ in the center and saints and angels lined up on either side, turning toward Him in prayer. The Greek word means "supplication."

Desert Fathers Christians who went into the wildernesses of Egypt and the Middle East to live dedicated lives of prayer, during the third through fifth centuries. The term includes Desert Mothers as well.

Dormition The feast of the death of the Virgin Mary, observed on August 15. The word means "falling-asleep."

Epiphany The feast of the baptism of Christ in the Jordan, observed on January 6. The Greek word means "showing forth" or "manifestation." Also called "Theophany."

Eucharist The worship service in which bread and wine become the Body and Blood of Christ. Eucharist means "thanksgiving." The Eucharist is served every Sunday in every Orthodox church. The service most frequently used is the Divine Liturgy of St. John Chrysostom, the core of which was assembled and composed in the fourth century.

festal Having to do with a feast. The feasts of the church year are the annual observances of events in Scripture and Church history.

Holy Doors Double doors in the center of an iconostasis, directly in front of the altar. These usually bear an icon of the

Annunciation, and smaller icons of the Evangelists of the four Gospels. Some call them "Royal Doors."

icon   The Greek word means "image." A representation of figures or events from the Bible or Church history, usually painted but sometimes executed in mosaic.

iconostasis   A screen between the main body of a church and the altar area, which holds icons.

kontakion   Originally a sermon in verse, running to many stanzas, and commemorating a person or event on the liturgical calendar. Now only the opening verse is generally used, so that in use a kontakion is much like a troparion (see below).

Lent   The forty-day period of preparation and fasting before Pascha is called Great Lent; it is followed by Holy Week, which ends with Pascha. The fast period before Pascha is called "Great Lent." Lesser Lents occur at other times of the year, for example before Christmas ("Nativity") and the Dormition.

mandorla   An oval or elliptical halo of light around the entire body.

Nativity The usual Orthodox term for Christmas.

orans The early Christian posture of prayer, standing with the hands uplifted.

Pascha The usual Orthodox term for Easter.

skete A community of monks that is a dependency of another monastery. Named after the community of Desert Fathers at Scetis in Egypt.

tesserae Small squares of glass or stone used in making a mosaic image.

Theophany Like "Epiphany," a name for the feast of the baptism of Christ in the Jordan, observed on January 6. The Greek word means "showing forth of God" or "manifestation of God."

Theotokos The usual Orthodox title for the Virgin Mary. The Greek word means "Birthgiver of God."

troparion The general term for a short hymn honoring a person or event commemorated on that day of the liturgical calendar.

Uncreated Light The light which belongs to God alone, as opposed to ordinary earthly light. Also called the "light of Mt. Tabor," the light that shown forth from Jesus at His Transfiguration.

venerate A person greets an icon by venerating it. He makes the sign of the cross on his head, chest, and shoulders with his right hand, perhaps with a bow to touch the floor, then kisses the icon on the hands or feet of the person depicted. He may light a candle and leave it before the icon, or stand a short while in prayer, and may conclude with another cross and bow. The central act of the veneration is the kiss.

RESOURCES

St. Isaac of Syria Skete offers all the icons in this book and hundreds more, laminated onto wood and in many sizes. You can contact them at:

St. Isaac of Syria Skete
25266 Pilgrim's Way
Boscobel, WI 53805
Ph 800-81-ICONS
www.skete.com

Another good source for laminated icons is Holy Transfiguration Monastery.

Holy Transfiguration Monastery
278 Warren Street
Brookline, MA 02445
Ph 800-227-1629
www.thehtm.org

Hand-painted icons can also be made to order. Your local Orthodox church may be able to direct you to iconographers who live nearby.

FOR FURTHER READING

Forest, Jim. *Praying With Icons*. Maryknoll,NY: Orbis Books, 1997. A rich volume of essays on many aspects of icons, well-illustrated.

St. John of Damascus. *Three Treatises on the Divine Images*. Crestwood, NY: St. Vladimir's Seminary Press, 2003. This book presents three works by the most significant ancient theologian on the topic of icons.

Martin, Linette. *Sacred Doorways: A Beginner's Guide to Icons*. Brewster, MA: Paraclete Press, 2002. This unique book combines a deep reverence for icons with an artist's understanding of their physicality and the process of their material birth.

Nouwen, Henri J.M. *Behold the Beauty of the Lord*. Notre Dame, IN: Ave Maria Press, 1987. This devotional classic offers in-depth meditations on four significant icons.

Ouspensky, Leonid and Vladimir Lossky. *The Meaning of Icons*. Crestwood, NY: St. Vladimir's Seminary Press, 1999. A beautiful edition of the 1952 classic, a large-format book with a text that is both scholarly and profound.

You can reach me at this address.
Please keep me in your prayers. www.frederica.com